The Mindful Eating Bible

The Secret Mind Hack For Ending Binge Eating And Emotional Eating, Rediscovering A Healthy Relationship With Food, And Ending Your Life-long Battle With Weight Loss

Sara Oakley

Table of Contents

The Mindful Eating Bible	1
Table of Contents	2
Introduction	4
Chapter One: Listen to Your Body	10
Chapter Two: Eat Only When You Are Physically Hungry	23
Chapter Three: Eat at Set Times and Places	36
Chapter Four: Choosing Nutritious Food	47
Chapter Five: Eat Rather Than Multitask	58
Chapter Six: Consider the Food Source	68
Chapter Seven: Emotional Eating	78
Chapter Eight: You Can Change Your Thinking	90
Chapter Nine: Enjoy Eating When It's Time to Eat	102
Chapter Ten: You Are a Mindful Eater	117
Final Words	134

© Copyright 2018 - All rights reserved.

It is not legal to reproduce, duplicate, or transmit any part of this document in either electronic means or in printed format. Recording of this publication is strictly prohibited and any storage of this document is not allowed unless with written permission from the publisher except for the use of brief quotations in a book review.

Introduction

In *The Mindful Eating Bible Outline: The Secret Mind Hack For Ending Binge Eating And Emotional Eating, Rediscovering A Healthy Relationship With Food, And Ending Your Life-long Battle With Weight Loss,* you will discover that it is possible for you to have peace with food. Many people often feel like food is the enemy. Everyone needs to eat, but the problem is knowing when to begin eating and when the meal should end. After reading this book, the answers should be clear to you. After practicing mindful eating, you will no longer have to wonder if you are eating the right amounts of food, or if you are eating too much. You can have confidence in your new-found ability to make judgment calls concerning your eating habits without having to rely on counting calories and fat grams.

Throughout this book, you will learn that there are techniques to mindfulness that will help you to change the way you think about food. Not only will you learn ways to stop overeating, but you will also discover that you can enjoy eating at the appropriate time without feelings of guilt. You can have joy over your relationship with food rather than guilt and self-loathing. Guilt-free eating experiences are awaiting you. You were meant to enjoy food. It was just not meant to be an obsession that controls every aspect of your life.

Is it possible for you to enjoy your meal times yet not be pulled by the magnetic force of food? I can tell you that, without a doubt, it is possible. As a matter of fact, it is a guarantee if you simply follow the mindfulness techniques laid out in this book. Each chapter contains small steps you need to take to be a mindful eater. These non-judgmental steps will guide you to a path of freedom laid out just for you. You will be encouraged to observe your own eating habits, form an assessment, then make any necessary corrections. No guilt or shame is needed.

Mindfulness will put food in its proper perspective. No longer will you dwell on your next meal after having just finished the last one. You will learn to focus on food while you are eating rather than attempt to multitask so you can feel satisfied with the amount of food that you have eaten. It is possible that you have forgotten how certain foods taste. Mindful eating will help you rediscover the joy of eating. The techniques discussed in this book will help you focus your thoughts away from food until you are truly hungry again. The process will bring joy not only to your eating, but also to your entire life.

You will no longer obsess over every bite of food that you put in your mouth. Obsession is not your friend. Mindful eating will help you to determine when you should eat and when you have had enough. Get ready to embark on a new journey in your life in which you will be able to enjoy every part of your life, including eating, yet you will not be controlled by food. How liberating it will be to walk free from the pull of the kitchen and refrigerator!

Do you find yourself obsessing over food when you are not the slightest bit hungry? While you are on the job, or working at home, does your mind dwell on the contents of your next meal? You are not alone in the obsession with food and eating. Many other individuals have the same struggle, and many people have discovered that the key to unlocking the door to freedom is learning to eat mindfully. Others have discovered this life-changing strategy that will help you lose weight and remain in control of your thoughts and feelings toward food.

Why is it that every event that we attend must have an endless buffet of food that not only lacks nutritional value, but leaves you feeling ill and guilt-ridden after eating it? Baby showers, family reunions, parties, shopping events, and so many more are centered on a table of edible goodies for which you have no need, particularly if you ate before attending. You will be given ways to escape the temptation of eating when your body is not physically hungry no matter where you are. Enjoy social events without the anxiety of worrying about food.

The obsession with having food at every event often leads to binging. You are in such a habit of constantly putting something in your mouth that to go without it causes you to panic. What if you are unable to get to your snacks? What if it is close to noon, but you are in a meeting to which there is no end in sight? You will discover that you have nothing to fear. Food is not meant to be your companion but rather something you enjoy that happens to give you sustenance. Mindful eating gives you the peace you need to enjoy eating without guilt once again.

If you are late to get your meals, do you find yourself eating rapidly and pouring as much into your mouth as possible? If you missed a meal throughout the day, do you find yourself binging at home that evening? Do you wait until no one is watching to consume more than hearty amounts of your favorite food? The techniques in this book are for you. There is hope. Change can be more than a possibility. It can be a fact that you establish.

Does your binging lead to bouts with depression? You know that eating large amounts of any food is not good for you. You are harming your body, yet, you seem unable to stop yourself. Knowing that it is time to stop eating, you still continue. The food just tastes so good, or, it seems to be temporarily meeting a need for you. Some of these needs could be the need for love, fulfillment, appreciation, and affirmation. You will learn to stop looking to food for these needs and find fulfillment in other productive ways.

After binging, do you face a deep sense of depression and tremendous guilt for days? When you think about how much food you have consumed, or, how much weight you have gained over a period of time, do you find yourself plunging into hopeless despair? You are not alone. I have been exactly where you find yourself now. Unfortunately, hopelessness is not a foreign feeling to many of us. However, you do not have to remain without hope. You can be free from depression and guilt. Mindful eating will be just the tool you need to begin repair to your body and emotions.

You know that you must regain control of your eating habits, but you have no idea how to begin. Keep reading, and you will gain a vast store of knowledge and the wisdom to apply it. Your desperate search for answers has finally ended. You are holding the answer in your hands. Keep reading to get all you need.

In the following chapters, you will discover that you simply need to change the way you think about and relate to food. The answer really is that simple, but it is not altogether easy. Mindfulness takes time and requires a great deal of focus. It is a step-by-step process, but this book will guide you every step of the way.

What does it mean to be mindful? Although the meaning of the word will be discussed in great detail in the following chapters, the simple definition of mindfulness is to simply be aware or conscious of something. This book is meant to raise awareness concerning eating habits and the types of food choices many people make. The following chapters are not meant to dictate every bite you put in your mouth, but simply to serve as a guide to make you aware of your habits, then implement mindful strategies to change the way you think about food. When you change your thinking, you change your life.

If you are ready to change the way you eat and think about food, please keep reading. If you are ready to change your life, read on to discover the detailed concepts of mindfulness. You cannot afford to procrastinate another minute. Keep reading and implement the strategies given. Change the way you think about food, and you will change the way you eat. In addition to changing the way you eat, you will change your thinking in other areas as well. Your life is about to change.

Chapter One: Listen to Your Body

Our bodies are pretty amazing! They are designed perfectly to give us specific signals as to when it is time to refuel with nourishing food. For some reason, we do not trust our bodies to let us know when they need food, water, and rest. Simply listening to our bodies will save us loads of health issues. When you are tired, it is time to rest. When you are thirsty, you need something to drink. When your stomach is empty, you need to eat. When you begin to feel the food in your stomach, it is time to stop eating.

You can trust your body to give you signals that indicate exactly what it needs. Your nervous system was designed to send messages back and forth between our brain and your body. When you touch an object that is too hot, signals are sent throughout your body to your hand. The hot and burning sensation your hand feels lets you know you need to let go of that object. It is the same with food. Your body signals your brain when your stomach is empty. Next, you will receive a loud and clear message that it is time to eat. Know that you can trust your body.

Often, there is a hollow, empty feeling below the rib cage that is sometimes accompanied by a growl. The uncomfortable feeling can usually be attributed to physical hunger. A satisfied feeling will usually become apparent to let one know that is time to stop eating. Mindful eating practices teach you to become aware of and listen to these signals.

Hunger Signals

The hunger sensation is just below the rib cage. If there is a growl or another sensation further down, that is an indication of another issue rather than hunger. Sometimes, people will experience a growl in the lower part of the stomach because the digestive system is processing your last meal. True hunger will be felt in the upper portion of the stomach.

It is also important to note that a burning sensation can be experienced in the upper portion of the stomach that can be attributed to acid reflux or heartburn rather than hunger. Time will usually make the difference known. It will not hurt to wait a few minutes before eating to make sure you are truly hungry. I have heard mindfulness experts often say, "When in doubt, do without." If you wait long enough, true hunger will become obvious. You will not have to search for it.

Another signal that will often accompany hunger is a slight headache. A tense pressure on both sides and even on top of the head are the type that accompanies hunger. When a headache comes with hunger, that signals a drop in the blood sugar. Other types of headaches are not typically associated with hunger. You do not have to eat every time you have a headache. Simply think about the time of your last meal and the type of headache that is bothering you.

If you find yourself becoming irritable for no reason, and it has been several hours since your last meal, that is a good indication that your body is experiencing hunger. A drop in the blood sugar will cause irritability. If you are not in a place where you can eat when this occurs, try taking a few sips of a sugary drink, or eating a cracker until you can get a meal. Please note that every time you feel irritation is not a signal that you must eat right away

Some people have found that dizziness is a sign of physical hunger. There are some who might not get a stomach growl or even feel an empty sensation below the rib cage, but they will feel dizzy or light-headed several hours after eating. As previously discussed, a drop in blood sugar levels can bring on some uncomfortable symptoms.

Lack of concentration can be another symptom of physical hunger. When the body needs refueled, energy levels along with blood sugar levels can decrease which affects concentration. If you are working on an important task and notice that you are having difficulty concentrating, it could be an indication that your body is ready for its next meal. The signals will become more obvious as time passes.

One final symptom of physical hunger can be nausea. Although nausea is associated with vomiting or other stomach ailments, it can be a sign that you are simply hungry. If that is the case, the nausea will be gone soon after eating. Make sure you eat slowly in these cases. Eating too rapidly can irritate the problem.

Hunger signals vary with each individual. It is important for you to begin the process of mindful eating by observing your body's signals when it is close to meal time. After a few times of paying attention, your signals should become apparent to you. Some people experience a headache and lightheadedness while others simply feel a hollow sensation in the stomach with or without a growl. Sometimes trial and error will be the approach. Do not panic if you have some error in the trial process. The errors will be a learning experience for you. If you are truly practicing mindful eating, you will notice some weight loss after a period of time. If you do not lose weight, or you gain weight, you need to reassess your hunger signals.

Signals for Fullness

As important as it is to be aware of true hunger, recognizing fullness is of equal importance. How can you know when it is time to stop eating? Some misconceptions concerning fullness must be settled before you will be able to find the point of satisfaction. Fullness is not being stuffed. It is a polite and pleasing feeling in your stomach after you have eaten a reasonable portion of food. When you begin to feel the food in your stomach, you will know that you are close to satisfaction.

When eating, take your time. Do not shovel the food into your mouth and down your throat as fast as it will go. Eating too fast will cause you to miss the fullness signal and overeat. Slowing down, taking smaller bites, and actually tasting the food will help you feel more satisfied. There is no rush. Our fast-paced lives have us in the habit of doing all things in a hurry. Slowing down will help with stress as well as eating.

As you approach fullness, you will begin to feel the food in your stomach. It is a good idea to stop eating for a few moments to assess where you are as far as fullness is concerned. You will notice that food begins to lose its taste to you as you reach the point in which you need to stop.

You should stop eating before you feel completely full. If not, you will go beyond full and end up being stuffed which is not where your stomach needs to be. As a matter of fact, stopping before you feel completely full is better because it takes the stomach a few minutes to send a signal to the brain that you have had enough. You should stop before you feel completely full if you are struggling with eating slower.

Some mindful eaters rate their physical hunger and fullness level by a scale of 1 to 10 with 1 being dizzy, nauseous, and shaky from hunger, and 10 being sick/binge eating full. Here is an example of such a scale.

The Hunger/Fullness Scale

1. Dizzy/Nauseous/Shaky
2. Irritable/Headache
3. Growling Stomach
4. First Sign of Hunger
5. Satisfied
6. Physically Full
7. Slightly Uncomfortable
8. Need to Unbutton Pants
9. Thanksgiving Full

10. Binge fullness/sickness

Most of the time, you need to be between 2-5, or 3-5. Of course, no one is perfect, but once you pass the point that you should be in either direction on the scale, observe and make a mental note of the way your body felt. Next time, you will be able to recognize your hunger and fullness a bit quicker.

Beating yourself up when you make mistakes in mindful eating is not helpful. It will only exacerbate your problem. Observing your mistakes, then taking steps to correct them is productive. You will obtain more positive results. Correcting your mistakes instead of berating yourself for them is a part of the mindfulness process.

When people first begin mindful eating, they will often find hunger rather easily but struggle with finding fullness. Too often, they will pass by satisfaction and end up uncomfortable. It is easy to become discouraged at this point, but it is important to be mindful, or aware, of the problem then focus on ways it can be solved. For example, did you eat too fast? Were you distracted in some way that kept you from truly tasting and enjoying your food? It is important to enjoy the foods you are eating. While it is essential to eat nutritious foods, it is equally important to choose the nutritious food that you enjoy. Some of these details will be discussed more fully in other chapters.

One of the steps to eating mindfully is to avoid counting calories or fat grams. You no longer need to weigh and measure your food. Your stomach is the size of your fist, not completely closed, of course. While you do not have to only eat a fistful of food at each meal (different foods have different volumes), you do need to simply pay attention to your portion sizes. A fistful of food might not be enough, but I believe it is safe to say that two plates full would be more than you need.

Take Small Steps to the Goal

Mindful eating is not a feat that can be accomplished instantly. After all, Rome was not built in a day. With that being said, it is as if you are building a house in this process When building a house, you must have a good, strong foundation If not, everything you build after the foundation will crumble. It is the same with mindful eating. You must start with small steps. Chances are if you wake up and say to yourself, "Today, I am going to eat mindfully", yet, take no steps to prepare yourself, you will not succeed.

If you are running a marathon, you do not need to take off at full speed. You have to pace yourself, or, you will wear out quickly. As a result, you will not be able to finish the marathon. When you begin mindful eating, take it one step at a time. Rather than look at the long journey you are taking, take one step at a time, and one milestone at a time. Before you know it, you will be able to see progress.

Additional Insight

When you are going to sit down and eat, ask yourself this: "Am I physically hungry?" If the answer is yes, proceed to choose food that you enjoy yet has good nutritional value. It is fine to have food that does not appear to have nutritional value occasionally, but it should be the exception, not the rule.

If you ask yourself about being truly hungry, and you find that the answer is that you are not truly hungry, assess the situation. What is the cause of you turning to food for an answer when it is not what you need. Are you bored? Do you have an emotion that is running rampant? Either way, food is not the answer.

Should boredom be your problem, find an activity that you enjoy doing, such as taking a walk, reading a book, calling a friend, or spending time with family. If you are emotional, assess what has been going on in your life, and why you are experiencing this emotion. Once you have figured out the reason for this raging emotion, address that issue.

If you take these steps on a consistent basis, you will find that food will lose its grip on you, and you will only be seeking out food when you need to satisfy the physical need of hunger. Food will be put into proper perspective. When this happens, you will have true peace and joy in your life.

When you are hungry, select the food you wish to eat. Put a small portion on a plate or in a bowl. To begin with, try to reduce your portions by half of what you would normally eat. Use a fork or spoon. It has been proved that eating with utensils slows down your pace of eating. When you eat slower, your chances of staying where you need to be on the hunger scale increases.

It can not be stressed enough that you must avoid self-loathing and using the club of self-condemnation to hammer yourself. Once again, you accomplish nothing this way. Self-assessment by observing your mistakes and correcting them will bring the results you desire.

I have found that writing certain statements of affirmation or motivation on index cards is a great help. I can refer to these throughout the day as reminders of where my focus should be. For example, I could write the following statement on an index card or sheet of paper: "My life is better when I set boundaries for food and eating."

Another statement could be this: "Food is a terrible friend. It will not truly comfort me. Any comfort I feel will be momentary, and I will soon be back where I started."

The issue of eating for the wrong reasons will be discussed in more detail in Chapter Two.

Food choices will be discussed in another chapter, but a little can be said now about the matter since food choices often affect hunger and fullness. Choosing protein-rich foods will help you stay full longer. Along with mindfulness, foods that keep you from becoming hungry as often will help keep your mind off eating in between meals. Find protein-rich foods that you enjoy. Mindful eating does not have to be torture.

In addition to eating protein-rich foods, drinking water can often delay hunger for a short time, plus, it is good for you. Water cleanses your body of toxins and is great for the metabolism. Water is also good for your kidneys and liver.

In between meals, have a plan of action in case you are tempted to nibble, or have a binge when your stomach is not empty. One of the steps you can take to occupy your mind is to engage in activities that you enjoy - take a walk, or simply get out of the house and go visit a friend or relative. If you need to, read the statements that you have written that were previously discussed. Not having a plan of action will result in a setback. By now, you should be making progress so a setback is not something that you want; however, a setback does not mean that you should give up. Never give up on your journey to mindful eating.

When you have a setback, it is important to evaluate the cause. Did you have negative emotions that you had not dealt with that surfaced? Is there another reason that you believe food is the answer to all problems? Sometimes, it can be painful, but facing these issues will eliminate emotional eating.

Part of mindful eating is being mindful of the thoughts and activities in which you are engaging while in between meals. If your thoughts are drifting toward the leftovers in the refrigerator, it is time to shift your thoughts in another direction. Find something to occupy your thoughts.

Linda is at an after-hours office party at her job site. She has been practicing mindful eating, and she has done well. People have even commented on her weight loss. The office party is the first event she has attended in a while. She is a little nervous because she is afraid that if she does not eat perfectly, she will be a failure and automatically resume old habits.

Before selecting her food, Linda realizes that she is hungry. She can feel a hollow, empty sensation just below her rib cage. Linda remembers a conversation she had with a life-coach who introduced her to mindful eating. Linda's coach had told her to select a small plate and choose the small portions of the foods Linda knew she would enjoy. The coach recommended that Linda avoid going back for seconds.

Remembering the advice, Linda follows it to the letter. Later, after Linda has finished eating, and she is comfortably full, a co-worker suggests getting a dessert. Linda politely refuses. The co-worker is insistent. Linda's mind begins to wander. One piece of cake would not hurt.

Linda still has the opportunity to stop at this point although her mind is slightly in the wrong direction. If Linda is satisfied physically, she does not need to eat anymore. Doing so could upset her stomach.

We all find ourselves in situations such as Linda's from time to time. It is important to be mentally prepared. There are times when we might have to disappoint someone else to do what is best for our bodies.

Chapter Summary

- Hunger is accompanied by a hollow, empty feeling under the ribcage. Tension headaches, dizziness, nausea, and irritability are also signals of hunger.
- Fullness is not being stuffed. It is a feeling of satisfaction and feeling the food in your stomach.
- Before eating, make sure you are truly hungry and not feeling overly emotional.
- Take small steps toward mindful eating. You will not reach the goal in one day.
- Have strategies in place to occupy your mind when you should not be eating.

In the next chapter, you will learn various strategies to determine the differences between physical and emotional hunger. You will also discover ways to combat emotional hunger.

Chapter Two: Eat Only When You Are Physically Hungry

Eating only when you are truly hungry sounds logical. It seems so easy. The concept is simple, but the process is far from easy. In fact, it is downright difficult if you are in the habit of eating for comfort. Distinguishing between physical and emotional hunger can be challenging when you first begin to practice mindful eating. You must be proactive, or you can easily find yourself eating for emotional reasons.

Finding and Fulfilling Physical Hunger

As discussed in the previous chapter, there are a few physical signals that can be used to determine if your hunger is physical or emotional. First, is your stomach empty? If so you will have an empty feeling below the ribcage that may, or may not, be accompanied by a growl. Second, you may get a tension headache. Next, you might become dizzy or lightheaded. Fourth, you can become irritable. Finally, you can experience nausea.

Once you know that you are hungry, and you are ready to sit down and eat, it would be wise to get only half the amount of food you usually serve yourself. Before mindful eating, you were used to eating large platefuls of food. You might have even eaten more than one large plateful of food. No matter the extent of overeating, mindfulness can change it. Eat food from a small plate if possible, and use utensils. Eating from a small plate limits the amount of food you can put on your plate while using utensils slows down your eating.

When you begin eating, take small bites, savoring the taste. Allow your taste buds to do their job. Your senses work wonderfully so put them to the test during eating. The senses work with the mind to help you begin to experience satisfaction or fullness. Do not rush this process. To eat mindfully is to take your time and enjoy your meal. If you rush your meal, you will not enjoy it as much, and you will feel deprived later as if you did not eat.

Put your fork or spoon down between bites. This pause will give you a moment to determine if you are approaching fullness. If people are eating with you, engage them in conversation. When it is time to stop eating, having someone to talk to makes the process easier.

If you need to lose a great deal of weight, you will find that your portion sizes will end up decreasing dramatically. Do not be alarmed nor sad. This is progress! You will be able to see how little you truly need, and you can be happy. Your life is about to change! Your mindset is changing! You are learning to eat mindfully which is better than a fad diet with little or temporary change. Mindful eating brings permanent results!

These steps were not easy for me to comprehend when I first began mindful eating practices. Much trial, error, and practice occurred before I got it right, and still, I made mistakes. If I can learn the process, so can you.

Although this book is about mindful eating, do not neglect exercise unless you have a physical limitation that prevents you from such activity. Exercise releases endorphins that cause you to feel energetic and lose the feeling of being lethargic. Exercise is a good remedy for depression as well.

Remember that your stomach is approximately the size of your loosely-clenched fist. Naturally, it will take more of some foods to satisfy you than others, depending upon density. The reference to your fist will give you a guide as to how much you should be eating. It is not a large amount, and you will feel so much better when you do not overeat. Your metabolism and brain will function better. You might even find that any negative issues you have had with your stomach will eventually be resolved. One lady, who practices mindful eating, revealed that once she began thinking about what she was eating and paying attention to the mindful eating concepts, she started noticing that she was getting good cholesterol readings. Her other medical tests came back showing her to be in good health.

Overeating puts an unnecessary burden on your stomach and the rest of your body. Having less food to digest will allow your body functions to work in other places which will improve the overall state of your health and well being. It might take more time than you would like, but with all these benefits, you will find yourself shedding those extra pounds. Overall, you will find yourself feeling great.

Boredom Eating

If you are bored, there are plenty of other activities that can keep you busy rather than eating. When you eat out of boredom, you are setting your body up to leave you with no energy as it must devote its resources to digesting extra food. Your mindset must be changed to look for other methods of occupying yourself. If you are a reader, keep plenty of reading material around to occupy you. If you have a cluttered room, work on decluttering when you are bored. If you love to write, get a journal and write. There are plenty of ways to occupy your mind when you are bored.

The concept of boredom is sometimes difficult to imagine because our lives are so fast-paced and busy. When we have moments of quiet and lack of activity, rather than enjoying the moment, we feel the need to fill the time with food rather than another enjoyable activity. In addition to being mindful of the food you are eating, another aspect of mindful eating is finding activities to occupy your mind when you should not be thinking about food. All of these steps are completely doable.

Physical Hunger Versus Emotional Hunger

Emotional hunger can disguise itself as physical hunger. It is deceitfully convincing. If you are an emotional person by nature, or if you have been through abuse or trauma that has caused your emotions to spin out of control, it is easy to develop an attachment to comfort food.

Unfortunately, if the emotional issues are not dealt with, you will have an additional problem-- weight gain!

There are certain clues that you can look for in order to tell emotional hunger from physical hunger. These clues are as follows:

- Emotional hunger comes suddenly while physical hunger comes gradually. If the urge to eat demands immediate satisfaction, or a sudden craving, it is most likely coming from your emotions.
- Emotional hunger results in mindless eating. If you have eaten a whole bag of chips or consumed more than half of a birthday cake before you are even aware of it, emotions are driving your appetite.
- Emotional hunger is never satisfied. Once you have finished binging, the only thing left for you is regret.
- Emotional hunger does not come from your stomach. Your craving will be in your mind with no physical symptoms.

Emotional triggers will be discussed in a later chapter.

Mindfulness Techniques for Emotional Hunger

When a craving for comfort foods comes, as it will if you are an emotional eater, be aware of the emotions you are experiencing when the cravings come. If necessary, write the details down in a private journal so you will have it to reflect on in the future. Dealing with negative emotions will be discussed later, but first, it is necessary to see if you can determine the types of emotions you are experiencing.

Once you have determined if you are craving certain foods when you are angry, and you want other types of food when you are sad, you will be aware of the negative emotions. Although you might not be ready to deal with the emotional trigger, you will at least be able to come up with a battle plan to keep you away from food when the emotions present themselves.

The following is an example of recognizing emotions that bring about food cravings: You come home one evening after having a horrible day at work. The boss just was not satisfied with any task you completed, yet he complimented your co-workers on a job well done. You believe he is being unfair. Normally, you would go find a pint of ice cream or a pan of brownies and eat away to comfort yourself. This time you are going to take a different approach.

First, you will acknowledge your emotions. Admit that you are angry with your boss. Whether or not you are entitled to that anger is another matter for another time. Admit that you just want to binge on some comfort food. Now, you are being honest with yourself which is a major step towards change.

Next, you decide that you are going to choose a more productive way to comfort yourself. You resolve to stay away from the kitchen until you have your emotions under control. Why not take a bath? If that does not comfort you, go for a walk and listen to your favorite music through your phone or iPod. Other steps you could take would be to talk to your spouse, a family member, or a good friend.

After taking that second step, you begin to feel more calm and peaceful. You will make a plan to deal with your boss in a productive way. Now, you are noticing that your stomach is growling and has an empty feeling. You can go to the kitchen and mindfully make wise food choices because you are no longer ruled by your emotions.

Of course, this is just one situation, but the concepts can be applied to a variety of scenarios. No matter what strong emotions you are feeling, you can choose to take comfort and deal with them in a healthy and productive way. Then, when you are truly hungry, you will enjoy a meal that you will not feel regret for later.

When to Stop

If you have not been practicing mindful eating very long, finding the point where you are full (not stuffed) is a challenge. As with finding hunger, there are different ways you can find fullness. This is a major step in the process because you are used to putting large volumes of food into your body without giving it a thought. In our fast-paced world, we are accustomed to doing everything in a hurry, including eating.

Unfortunately, eating in a hurry is a major hindrance to finding fullness. As stated before, it takes several minutes for the body to signal the brain that enough food has been taken into the stomach. If you eat too fast, the signal will still reach the brain, but only after you have already eaten too much.

Now that you know that it is a good idea to use a small plate and utensils. The eating environment will be discussed in later detail, but you must know that eating in an environment without distractions will help you to be relaxed with your meal. As a result, you will find yourself eating slower, taking smaller bites, and, most of all, find fullness very easily.

You should stop eating just as you begin to realize the food has filled your stomach about three-fourths of the way. This process will have to be practiced to be perfected. Sometimes trial and error is the way you learn. After all, mindfulness raises awareness. Raising awareness is one step to solve a problem, but it is not the entire solution. Once awareness has been raised, you can now begin to work on the changes.

Changes will begin to come to your eating habits when you begin to slow down and really taste the food. It is only then that you will realize just how much you have hurried through your meals rather than enjoying them. Habits can be broken, but it takes time, particularly if you have been in these habits for years.

Besides taking a smaller plate, it is wise to develop the boundary of refusing to go back for seconds unless you truly took too small of an amount of food when you first put it on your plate. This should be the exception, not the rule. Most of the time, when you go back for seconds, you end up eating too much.

Once you begin to feel the food nearly filling your stomach, get away from the food! Tell yourself that you can have more food later when you are hungry again. Training your mind to accept this important fact is a key to stopping at fullness because you will be more ready to give up the food if you do not think you will never again see or taste it.

When your meal is over, push the plate away from you, or, go put it in the sink. If the plate has leftover food on it, dispose of the food immediately so you are not tempted to eat your leftovers while you are washing dishes. Your body is not a garbage disposal. The body has been misused for too long where food is concerned so it is time to start treating it right. Since I have made these mistakes I can advise you without malice or judgment. I know what it is like to be caught in a cycle of disordered eating.

After the food is away from you, get away from the kitchen or other sources of the food quickly. Only return to the kitchen if you need to load the dishwasher, or hand wash your dishes. If you do enter the kitchen to clean, have a plan in place. Keep food put away and avoid leaving snacks laying out. Once you are accomplished at mindful eating, having snacks out on your kitchen counter might not be a problem, but, to begin with, you have to remove sources of temptation.

Now it is time to occupy your mind with an activity you enjoy. Maybe you enjoy spending time with your family, or, maybe you have been wanting to read a new book. Do you crochet, or do you write? Any enjoyable activity is fine as long as it does not involve food.

Important Points

Remember to keep track of your feelings and progress in a journal. You will have this to look back on to see your progress and encourage yourself when you feel discouraged. Reflection on what keeps you on the path to progress is productive and helpful. You will not know if you have reached your destination if you do not know how far you have traveled.

It is always important to note that when you get off track with mindful eating, you do not have to wait until "tomorrow" to begin again. Start over right away! Tell yourself that you will wait until you truly feel hunger before you eat again. It could be several hours or more if your last meal was large. Remind yourself that food boundaries are so good for you. Think about how energetic you feel when you eat less food.

Another possibility to consider is to find an accountability partner. This should be someone you trust for constructive criticism, yet someone who will encourage and motivate you. When you are accountable to another person, you are provided motivation to keep your mind on the right track where eating is concerned. You are not as likely to get off track when you have someone cheering you on.

Practical Examples

Jackie loves birthday cake. The leftover cake from her son's birthday party is in the refrigerator, and it seems to be calling her name. She is home alone. Her husband and son went on an errand so if she stuffed herself with cake, no one would know.

Walking to the kitchen, Jackie justifies her actions. She was not hungry, but how often did she get to have birthday cake? It had been a while so she felt she was entitled to a snack. One piece would not hurt.

Opening the refrigerator, Jackie pulls out the cake and sits it on the counter. She looks in the kitchen drawers for the cake server. Finally, she gets herself a huge piece of cake. As she is getting ready to take the first bite, the phone rings. By the time Jackie takes the call and hangs up, she has lost the desire to eat the cake.

Had Jackie been truly hungry, she would still want to eat. She could have chosen a small piece of cake, or better still, chosen a healthier snack had she been physically hungry. Since she was not hungry, the phone call saved her.

You might not be saved by a phone call, but you can choose to put the food away if you are not truly hungry and come back to eat when you truly need to. The mindful eater is aware of the body's signals, and if the body is not calling for food, the mindful eater can turn it away.

Barbara loves pizza. Her husband brought home pizza after work since he passed the new pizzeria in town on his way home. Barbara was enjoying the aroma, and she truly was hungry. Sitting down with her husband, she asked him about his day and made conversation while eating one slice. Although Barbara felt completely satisfied, the temptation to grab another piece of pizza was strong. Before she knew it, Barbara found herself reaching for that second piece. To her horror, she ate a third piece before she knew what happened.

This scenario is all too familiar to me. I have overeaten many times knowing that I was past the point of enough. A mindful strategy is the key to getting past this obstacle.

When Barbara realized she was satisfied after the first piece, she could have removed the pizza from where she was. Another step she could have taken was to excuse herself from the table, then, return after she felt more in control. There is always a way to escape temptation. Mindful eating will help you find the way.

Chapter Summary

- Physical hunger is in the stomach, just below the ribcage.
- Use utensils and small plates.
- Emotional hunger is brought on suddenly while physical hunger comes gradually.
- Emotional hunger brings food cravings.

- Emotional hunger is never satisfied.
- Emotional hunger is not physical.
- Stop eating before the stomach is completely full.
- Find something to keep you occupied.
- Consider an accountability partner.
- You can always eat later.
- If you have a setback, start over right away.

In the next chapter, you will learn about setting times and places in which to eat.

Chapter Three: Eat at Set Times and Places

When waiting for hunger, it is not always possible to eat at the exact same time every day; however, your body will adjust to approximate times. The body requires routine and having this routine will have your body ready for meals at particular times. You should also have a certain place in mind to use for your meals such as the dining room table. Having a time and a place will help your mindful eating to be more meaningful. If possible, avoid eating in the same room where there is a television or desktop computer. Other devices should be removed from the room while eating.

Sit While Eating

It is not a good idea to eat while standing up. When you are standing, it is as if you are ready to take off so you are not truly relaxed in a manner that will allow you to enjoy your meal. Sitting suggests being comfortable, and you should be comfortable with eating. Standing will cause you to pay less attention to what you are eating which will result with overindulgence.

Sit at a table if possible. When you sit on your sofa to eat, you tend to focus on television or another distraction that keeps you from truly tasting and enjoying your food. As a result, you will feel deprived and be tempted to eat when your body has no need for food.

The area in which you are eating should be free from distractions. Turn off the television and put your phone away. If you talk to anyone, it should be your family or the person sharing the meal with you. Eating with others actually helps with mindful eating. You can concentrate on the conversation when tempted to eat more than necessary. When you know you have had enough, push your plate away from you. Throw your napkin over the food so it is out of your sight. The further the food is from you, the easier it is for you to avoid nibbling and other mindless eating.

Mindfulness involves being aware and absorbed in the moment. You need to be totally involved in your meal time. As you become aware of issues that preoccupy your mind when you are eating, you can make adjustments and move distractions and focus your mind on what you are doing.

When you are eating alone, practice keeping your focus on what you are doing. It is often tempting to allow your mind to wander when alone and quiet, but you can turn this to your advantage. Use the quiet to focus on the tastes and textures of your food. What foods feel best in your mouth? You might begin making observations about various foods that you did not notice at other times.

The Place You Eat

As previously discussed, it is best to eat at a table when at all possible, but wherever you choose to eat, it should be a place free from distractions such as the television, computer, or cell phone. Many people eat on the sofa or recliner while watching television or texting on the cell phone. If you use your sofa for watching television or texting, you should not use these to eat. The place you choose should be the place you will use most of the time, and it should be a place free of distractions.

Being free from distraction cannot be stressed enough. The distractions are the reasons that we have so many food issues. Our minds have been focused on dozens of other activities while eating. We seldom taste our food because we are not focusing on the food, or we are eating too fast without even chewing. We must relearn the lost art of enjoying food. It will prevent us from overeating due to feeling deprived.

My words are not meant to be a club with which to beat you. Awareness is simply the goal in this section, along with some strategies to help you reach your goals. If you want your weight loss to be permanent, then it is a permanent change that must take place. No one can keep doing the same thing and expect different results.

Mindfulness One Meal at Time

Once again, if you have not been practicing mindful eating for a very long time, or if you have just started, try taking small steps to achieve your goals. Do not attempt to complete everything in this book at one time. You will only become frustrated with the process.

To begin with, try eating mindfully at one meal per day. Next, try two meals per day. How long should you do this? The answer is different for everyone, but it is at your discretion. You alone know when you are ready to move. Be patient with yourself as you are learning. Time is what you need.

Mindful eating goes beyond your meal times. You have to practice being mindful of how much attention you give to food and thoughts of food in between meals. Awareness is a step towards change. When your thoughts drift to the leftover cake in the refrigerator, shift your focus to something else. You will have to repeat this process many times. Keep reminding yourself that you can eat later when you are hungry. You might have to say, "Food is not the boss. I am."

Mindful Eating Requires Patience

Patience is a required virtue for mindful eating. The practice is one that is moment-by-moment and day-by-day. A person who is impatient by nature will have to practice patience along with mindful eating. The one you will be most tempted to lose patience with will be yourself. Give yourself some grace. You are in a learning process.

When someone plants seeds for flowers, the seeds have to remain in the ground for a time before the flowers bloom. A caterpillar does not become a butterfly immediately. A baby is not born knowing how to walk and run. These are all processes that require time and patience, some of our most precious commodities. Mindful eating is a process. It has to be given time and attention for you to see results.

Bad eating habits did not develop in one day. It took time for past actions to become a habit. With that being said, you must give mindful eating time to work. Be patient with yourself as well as the process. Often, I would lose patience with myself through the process, but I found that it is better to forgive myself for shortcomings, then, try again. My outlook became more positive through the process, and yours will too.

Hungry But No Time to Eat

Unless you are a diabetic, if you are physically hungry but not in a place where you can get something to eat, you are not in any danger. Diabetics will usually have some type of healthy snack on hand for an emergency, but under normal circumstances, your discomfort will just last for a few minutes. The gnawing feeling will leave for a period of time. Usually, it returns in thirty to forty-five minutes so focusing your thoughts on the task you are completing will help.

If you find that you get nauseated when it is past time for you to eat, try keeping some crackers to nibble on. Two or three will be all you will need to take away hunger pangs until you are able to eat. If available, a few sips of some type of caloric drink will help.

A mindful eater learns not to panic if no food is on-hand right away when hungry. It might take time, but food can always be found. The food will taste better when you are truly hungry, and it will be worth the wait.

One of the disadvantages of being ravenously hungry is that you will often eat too fast which will lead to overeating. Mindful caution is the order of the day. Remind yourself when you sit down to a meal, and you are ravenous that the food is not going anywhere. You can eat slowly and enjoy your food. Eating rapidly will not help. Eat slowly, sipping water or another beverage in between bites. You will find that you will begin to feel better.

Utensils are Useful

When you first practice mindful eating, using utensils, even for finger foods helps you to eat slower. If possible, cut your food up into smaller pieces. This will take some time, giving you a few moments to give thought to what you are eating. Put your fork or spoon down between bites as this will give you a moment to assess where you are with hunger. You will be able to determine if you are approaching fullness, or if you should eat more.

Some mindfulness experts suggest using chopsticks while eating. Others say it is a good idea to use your non-dominant hand to hold your utensils. For example, if you are right-handed, hold your utensils with your left hand. Eating this way could be uncomfortable at first, but think of how much you will slow down while you are eating.

The Non-Judgmental Approach

A great advantage of mindful eating is its non-judgmental approach. You are extending peace to yourself. Realizing that you will not be perfect in this process, you must allow yourself room for mistakes. Being non-judgmental is not allowing yourself to eat anything in sight, but it is learning from your mistakes rather than beating yourself up over them.

What good does it do to simply chide yourself for your mistakes? You will only become discouraged and give up before you find peace with food. Instead, when you find yourself overly fixated on food, simply remind yourself that you do not need to eat until you are hungry. When you eat beyond fullness, assess your circumstances to see what might have been going on around you to lead you to lose focus. Getting to the root of the problem rather than simply treating a symptom will bring such powerful, positive, and life-changing results.

Practical Examples

Beth has had a rough day. Her daughter has been sick, so, Beth has been with her at the Pediatrician's office. On the way home, Beth stopped to get her daughter something to eat at a fast food restaurant. Beth was not hungry, but she felt the need to get some ice cream for herself. After all, her day had been stressful.

She always worries when her daughter gets sick, and they had to wait for several hours at the doctor's office. This is enough to exhaust anyone. Beth believes ice cream will make her feel better. It certainly worked when she was a child. Anytime she had had a bad day when she was younger, her mother always brought her ice cream.

Once Beth and her daughter arrived home, Beth put her little girl down for a nap. She opens her pint of ice cream. Rather than scooping some out and putting it into a bowl, Beth gets a spoon and eats from the carton. Beth does not want to sit at the table so she just relaxes on the couch. Not only has Beth's daughter been ill, but Beth has had some financial issues so she continues dwelling on her problems while she is eating. Before she realizes it, Beth has eaten the entire pint of ice cream. To make matters worse, she does not feel the least bit satisfied. As a matter of fact, she feels sick from too much sugar.

Looking at this scenario, it would be easy to assume that Beth could just cry and lament over her mindless eating. Although crying, in and of itself, is not wrong, and she might need to release emotions, beating herself up will not help. After releasing emotions, Beth could take a step back and look at the downward spiral that led her to eating too much ice cream.

First of all, she was stressed out due to a long day with a sick child. Secondly, she could have made another food choice when she stopped to get food. Next, she could have put a little ice cream in a bowl and sat down at the table to eat it slowly providing that her stomach was empty. Had she not been hungry, she could have placed the ice cream in the freezer until she was hungry. After that, she needed to acknowledge the childhood memory. Although her mother had meant well, comfort through food starts many people down the path of disordered eating.

    Before eating, Beth could have taken a moment to ask herself why she was eating. Was she truly hungry? Or, was there a need she wanted to satisfy that had nothing to do with her body? Evidently, the need was more emotional than physical. Beth could have taken a brief nap since she was exhausted, or she could have found a relaxing activity such as her favorite book, television show, or a bubble bath. There are always options available when a person is tempted to eat outside of healthy boundaries.

    We will examine another example. Angela is cooking dinner for her family. She keeps sampling her spaghetti sauce to see how it tastes. As she is putting the finishing touches on her meal, she samples the garlic bread she has made along with some chips from a bag left out on the kitchen counter.

    By the time Angela gets dinner on the table, she is full. Angela knows that if she eats, she will be sick. The family comes to the table. After everyone has been served, the family begins eating. Despite the full feeling, Angela scoops some spaghetti on to her plate along with another slice of garlic bread. After all, it just would not be right to skip out on eating with the family.

There are several things that Angela could have done differently in this situation. One taste of her spaghetti sauce while cooking would have been fine. After that, she could have reminded herself that she could have more when she sat down to eat with her family. Instead of eating the chips, she could have put the bag away so she would not be tempted to nibble. Finally, when she realized that she was too full to eat dinner, she could have just chosen to sit down with the family and not eaten, and if asked, simply explained that she was not yet hungry.

Many people can relate to these examples. I recognize myself in each of these women. Daily struggles in life as well as preoccupation cause people to sometimes shovel food into their mouths without thinking. Once reality hits, it is easy to despair and wish one could do better. Mindfulness is not only to be exercised toward meals, it is also to be put into action during the in-between times.

Chapter Summary

- Eat when sitting.
- Eat at the dining room or kitchen table.
- Turn off the television, cell phone, and computer.
- Be free from all distractions.
- Be mindful - one step, one meal at a time.
- Be patient with yourself and the process.
- Learn from your mistakes.

In the next chapter, various food choices will be discussed.

Chapter Four: Choosing Nutritious Food

Another step in the mindful eating process is learning to choose nutritious foods. There is nothing wrong with having occasional sweet treats, or other non-nutritious treats. It becomes a problem when people believe they must have treats at every meal. Choosing nutritious food is to choose those foods that will keep you from becoming hungry again too quickly. Some foods might be pleasing to the taste buds, but they leave you feeling dissatisfied. While examining the different food groups, it is important to note that people need foods from all groups. Balance is the key.

Protein

Protein is important to every cell in your body. It is used to repair and build tissue. Protein is essential for bones, blood, muscles, cartilage, and skin. Your hair and nails are made of mostly protein. Protein will keep you sustained longer. You will not become hungry as quickly as you would eating other foods.

The body does not store protein as it does carbohydrates. That is why it is important for you to get enough protein on a daily basis; however, that does not mean that you should eat huge quantities of protein with every meal. Approximately 5-7 ounces per day is needed. When you eat mindfully, your body will respond to the foods you eat. If you eat too much of one type of food, your body will let you know because you will suffer some ill effects.

There are ways you can vary your protein intake to get what you need. The following foods contain sufficient amounts of proteins so choose some that you enjoy eating: seafood, eggs, peas, beans, nuts, seeds, turkey, beef, chicken, tuna, and salmon. Having a variety of foods that you eat will keep you from becoming unbalanced in your eating. You will feel more satisfied eating a variety of foods rather than just one type.

Dairy

Like any other food group, dairy should not be overdone, but you do need to have a sufficient amount of it. Dairy products are linked to bone health. Vitamin D provides calcium and phosphorus. Potassium is also provided by certain dairy products. There is protein in some dairy products so you can get protein and dairy in one food choice.

Dairy foods such as milk, cheese, butter, yogurt, cottage cheese provide nutrients you need. Some breakfast cereals are rich in these nutrients. There is enough of a variety that you should be able to choose something you enjoy.

Once again, please choose healthy portions of these foods. Neither underdoing nor overdoing are helpful in mindful eating. You must take a balanced approach in your food choices.

Sugar

As with all other food ingredients, moderation is the key. Often, human beings have a difficult time practicing moderation. More always seems better, but that is not always the case. Mindfulness puts the idea of "more" into perspective. With mindful eating, you realize that you can have a moderate amount of most food types. There are times when you do not need them, then, there are times when a little is acceptable.

Many nutritionists believe that white refined sugar is the source of health problems. In some cases, that is true. In other cases, going to extremes to eliminate sugar from one's diet can cause more stress than it relieves. Some experts recommend substituting honey for white sugar. Once again, whatever your source of sweetener, moderation is the key to healthy eating.

A great deal of controversy has been present over artificial sweeteners. Many people use them in their tea, coffee, or other drinks because they believe they do not need the extra calories of a natural sweetener. Of course, diabetics often turn to this source because of their own health issues.

Whatever source of sugar you use and how often you use it should be a decision in which you have practiced mindfulness. Assess how too much sugar makes you feel. Personally, when I have ingested too much sugar, I often feel tired or irritable. A mindful eater notices how certain foods make her feel and makes needed adjustments accordingly.

Carbohydrates

Carbohydrates do not come without a bit of controversy, particularly in the health world. There are health experts who believe you should limit your carb intake. The South Beach Diet and the Atkins Diet have been popular as well as convincing. According to these diet programs, limiting your carb intake will turn your body into a fat burning machine. The problem is that carbs are needed for energy.

There are two types of carbohydrates: simple and complex. Simple carbohydrates are those that are found in table sugar, fruits, fruit juices, honey, and dairy products. Complex carbohydrates are also known as starches. Bread, crackers, pasta, rice, corn, peas, sweet potatoes, and white potatoes are sources of complex carbohydrates.

As with any other food product, moderation is key. Once again, mindful eating comes in with assessing how certain foods make you feel after you have eaten them. If a particular food drains you of energy, you might need to eat less of it. If you feel great after eating a certain type of food, you know that it has just what your body needs.

The Temporary Comfort of Comfort Foods

When you are not practicing mindful eating, there might be certain foods that you look to when you are in need of consolation. For a moment, it feels great to eat these foods; however, you do not feel comforted later. Some people look to sweets for comfort while others look to salty foods such as potato chips. In moderation and on certain occasions, these choices can be fine, but when they are being used to soothe hurt feelings or cheer up a depressed person, the comfort is, at best, temporary.

Human beings were not meant to find comfort in food. Comfort can be found in our families and friends as well as practicing thankfulness. When you think about what you have rather than what you do not have, you can find long-lasting comfort.

What is Considered to be a Comfort Food and Why

The main types of comfort food are the ones that are considered "junk food", but not all comfort foods are limited to this type. Any type of food that triggers a good memory from childhood or other pleasant times in your life is a comfort food. This explains why people turn to these various foods when they are going through stressful situations.

Some of these foods could be chocolate cake, lasagna, mashed potatoes, turkey, dressing, pizza, and many more. Memories are often triggered by these foods that bring back a pleasant feeling. Naturally, people will lean toward these foods when they feel insecure, or are facing a traumatic situation.

While it is not wrong to eat these foods in moderation, the need to turn to a food for comfort must be addressed. Dealing with the emotion that leads to the desire for the comfort food will help diminish your overwhelming desire for it. Emotions that lead to overeating will be discussed in another chapter.

Nutritious Foods Sustain Longer

If your life is as busy as mine is, you might find that it is much faster and convenient to turn to finger foods or comfort foods than it is to take the time to eat something that might sustain you longer. Although it takes a little extra time, the benefits of choosing foods that sustain you longer are invaluable. The extra time spent choosing or preparing these foods will be worth the time spent on the process.

When a food sustains you longer, you go longer without being fixated on what you are going to eat next. Cravings are reduced, and you will find that you feel great. Mindful eaters look for opportunities to choose foods that best serve their bodies and overall well being.

Before the sustaining foods are discussed, you might be surprised to find that water can help sustain you. Often, thirst is mistaken for hunger. Drinking a glass of water can satisfy what is perceived as hunger.

There are a variety of foods that will keep you full longer. Popcorn, eggs, vegetables, cottage cheese, and healthy fats such as almonds, walnuts, and pistachio nuts are some that will keep you from feeling hungry so quickly after a meal. As with other types of food, there is enough of a variety to keep you from feeling limited in your choices.

Eating for Both Enjoyment and Nutrition

It has been said that you can not have your cake and eat it too, but that saying is not always true. Sometimes you can. There are times to choose certain foods over others, but there are times to choose the foods you really love. Sometimes the food you love can be the best of both worlds. It is important to choose foods you do enjoy eating and eat those in moderation. If not, you could be tempted to return to binging.

A mindful eater is aware of the foods that taste good, yet, they still have great nutritional value. The mindful eater appreciates those foods, but the mindful eater also knows that, from time to time, she can eat something she loves that does not have nutritional value. She just has to remember that she cannot be controlled by foods with little nutritional value.

Foods that Affect Moods

Vitamin D has the quality of an antidepressant. This vitamin can be obtained through sunlight, but some foods contain the Vitamin D that you need. Mushrooms, milk, and beef contain Vitamin D. Dark chocolate has been known to reduce emotional stress.

Totally eliminating carbs can increase depression in some people. The reason for this is because carbs release tryptophan which causes more serotonin to be released in the brain. Serotonin is essential to regulating one's moods.

Often, choosing nutritious foods not only affects us physically but mentally as well. If these common food choices can boost your mood, why not give them a try? An elevated mood is an additional perk to mindful eating.

Practical Tips for Making the Choice

Diana loves sugary foods, particularly cookies and doughnuts because they are so convenient. She can pick them up and hold them in her hand as she goes about her routine. The problem is that Diana has started noticing that she feels sluggish throughout the day. At one time, she had enough energy to get accomplish all of her daily tasks and not feel exhausted. Now, it is all she can do to get through half the day without feeling as if she needs a nap.

To begin with, Diana attributes her problem to age. After all, she is in her early forties, and she is not getting any younger. She operates under this assumption until she overhears some co-workers talking about how too much sugar can affect one's energy level.

Little by little, Diana began replacing her cookies and doughnuts with other choices such as various fruits. From time to time, she still indulges in one cookie or one doughnut, but most of the time, she chooses the fruit. Once she took the time to cut it up, Diana noticed that the fruit was convenient too.

After she developed this habit, Diana began noticing that she was regaining her previous energy level. Diana no longer felt as if she could not make it through the day. She found that she did not even need a nap. Instead, she enjoys her daily routine and feels wonderful!

Like Diana, perhaps you need to replace a few choices with something more sustaining that leaves you feeling great without forfeiting the taste. Whether it is replacing some of your sugary snacks with fruit, or your potato chips with carrot or celery sticks, small choices along the way can make the world of difference. Take the time to be mindful of how certain foods make your body feel.

When Becky was having her meals, she chose fast food often because she was usually in a hurry because of the demands of her job. It had become a comforting habit to stop either before or after work at her favorite fast food restaurant and purchase a hearty breakfast, or a burger and fries depending upon the time of day. She found herself looking forward to these stops.

The problem was that Becky was starting to notice that she looked and felt bloated. Noticing the swelling in her fingers, Becky realized she was retaining water. Rather than taking a diuretic, Becky decided to drink more water instead of soda. In just a matter of days, Becky noticed that the swelling in her hands had been reduced.

Since drinking water had made some improvements, Becky decided that she would begin preparing food at home to bring with her to work. She chose a baked potato over french fries. Sometimes, she indulged in an order of french fries, but it was a not a daily routine. Instead of burgers, Becky ate leaner meats having a burger from time to time. It was not long before Becky noticed that she was no longer bloated. She also felt better overall.

Like Diana and Becky, observe how certain foods make you feel. If you notice that you are bloated, or you just do not feel well, write down what you are eating. Make adjustments if necessary. Sometimes too much of a certain type of food can contribute to our well-being or lack thereof.

Chapter Summary

- You need a balance of various types of food.
- Comfort foods only bring temporary comfort.
- Nutritious foods sustain longer.
- You can eat for both enjoyment and nutrition.

- Certain foods can affect your moods.

In the next chapter, you will learn why you should eat rather than multitask.

Chapter Five: Eat Rather Than Multitask

Multitasking is a popular concept these days, but the effectiveness of it is questionable. There might be some projects in which you could get by with multitasking, but when you are eating, especially mindfully eating, multitasking is not a good idea. In this case, multitasking will cause you to fail at mindful eating. Mindful eating is to be free from distractions, and multitasking can be very distracting.

When eating, eat!

When you are sitting down to eat, and by now you should be sitting down for your meals, do not attempt to complete other tasks. Focus on the food during this time. At other times, your focus should not be on food, but when you are eating, you want to eat mindfully. Focusing on food at mealtimes brings satisfaction which will keep you from binging later. Multitasking will rob you of that satisfaction.

In our society, people have adjusted to having constant entertainment or constant mental stimulation. While this is not altogether wrong, there comes a time when you should just focus solely on what is at hand. When you are eating, eat. Put your phone away. Place it in another room if necessary. If there is a television or computer in your dining room, move them. I realize I sound extreme, but mindless eating is what causes many of our health problems. You can not continue doing things the way you always have and expect to achieve different results.

If you are eating and find yourself losing focus, you do not have to continue in that way. There are ways you can regain focus. Once you realize you are eating and trying to read your emails or texts, get up, take the phone or tablet to another room, then return to your plate reminding yourself that you need to enjoy your meal, or at the very least, the people who might be in your company.

When regaining focus, look at the food on your plate. Notice the different colors and varying textures. What is it that causes you to like this particular food? How does it feel when it is in your mouth? You will also notice that food tastes best when you are truly hungry. Food will seem to lose its flavor the closer you come to being full.

Medical experts have conducted research which confirms that when a person does not pay attention to her meal, she tends to overeat. When a person pays attention to her meal, she will eat less later on. These are the results you are looking for with mindful eating. It is important that you are successful with this step. It can affect your results later on.

In order to truly enjoy a meal, allow yourself at least twenty minutes to eat. Set a timer if needed. Do not rush. Developing the habit of eating slower will take time and practice. Take small bites and chew slowly. There is no rush. Some experts suggest using chopsticks or holding the utensils in your non-dominant hand.

Get to know the foods you eat. What health function will they serve for you? After all, that is why we eat. Of course, we enjoy the flavors and textures, but we are eating for sustenance. Awareness is vital. Does your favorite food provide you with any types of vitamins your body needs or help aid important body functions? If you do have a health issue, find out the types of foods that are good for combating that issue. There should be at least one that you would enjoy.

If you still find yourself becoming distracted during mealtimes, assess what you have been eating. Do you have a tendency to eat the same foods over and over? If so, it is possible that you are tired of that type of food without even realizing it. Try some new dishes. Eating a balance of proteins, carbohydrates, and fats will help your eating experience as well. Variety is the spice of life.

Eating alone is good when practicing mindful eating, but it is also good to have company you enjoy as well. This enhances your experience and keeps you from becoming bored. Eating in good company builds more positive experiences with food which leads to less of an unhealthy relationship with food. When you have a negative outlook on food, you tend to overeat, undereat, or develop some type of disordered eating. Your eating experience should be positive.

Give yourself permission to enjoy food! Due to weight and health issues that have resulted from the misuse of food, people tend to see food in a negative light. Doing so does not enhance your mindful eating experience. Food is meant to be enjoyed while you are having your meals.

Having a variety of foods available will balance your experience making it enjoyable.

Multitasking and Mindfulness Do Not Mix

When eating and trying to multitask at the same time, you are robbed of enjoyment. As stated previously, multitasking might work for some tasks, but eating is not one of them. There is no way you can be tasting your food and eating mindfully if you are focused on another task at the same time.

One of the main reasons for overeating for women is that they are hungry for something other than food. It could be rest, affirmation, relationships, or a variety of other needs. When women multitask, as many women often do, they are unaware of much of what they put into their mouths so they do not even realize they are overeating at times.

Mindful eating raises awareness. There are some people who discover that they have forgotten how good some foods taste because they are shoveling them down instead of taking time to really taste them. Once a person begins practicing mindful eating, she often finds that her eating experience changes dramatically. Mindless eating results from multitasking and robs the individual of joy and satisfaction. As a result, people become mindless to the fact that they are eating to fulfill something other than the physical appetite.

Many people who overeat do not necessarily have a food fetish. They are often looking for some type of fulfillment that they are not getting from other areas of their lives. Mindful eating not only raises awareness of the flavors and varieties of food you are missing, but mindful eating helps you to see that you might be stuffing your emotions with food or looking for some type of fulfillment that isn't even physical.

People who have busy lives are in such a habit of multitasking and taking little time to rest that these habits cannot help but spill over into their meal times. They have forgotten to simply take the time to taste their food. They have forgotten to slow down and enjoy a meal. Mindful eating raises this awareness. Hopefully, you see the importance of laying aside the distractions and focusing on eating when you eat. As a result, you will be able to focus on other tasks when you need to complete them.

Although you do not have to overanalyze all you do, you will find that mindful eating will lead to mindfulness in other areas of your life. Because you might be in such a habit of multitasking, all of your tasks and activities automatically cross over with each other, including eating. When you learn to separate these parts of your life and focus on each area as you are working in it, you will notice that you complete all of those tasks better which means you will eat better. As a result, you will break old habits and begin losing weight.

Regaining Focus

The phrase "when eating, just eat," sounds simple enough. The fact is, it can take time to do. All of the steps and processes in mindful eating are just that-- steps and processes. The changes you are looking to make will not happen in a day.

You have already begun the first step to regaining focus. Awareness is that step, and your awareness level has been raised. In each situation you are in with your eating, stay focused on your eating. If you notice that your focus is shifting, as it most likely will from time to time, you can turn your attention back to your eating simply by turning away from the distraction. If the distraction is your own thoughts, say out loud, "It's time to get back to eating." When you are in a deep train of thought, speaking something aloud disrupts the thought pattern. Now, you can easily refocus.

If the distraction is a book, a task, the phone, or another device, you know to remove those things immediately. Sometimes, we are interrupted by a knock at the door. If an emergency redirects your focus, that is not something that you can help. Simply regain focus as soon as possible, or, you might have to wait until the next meal. If so, do not worry. Life happens to us all. Get back on track at your next meal.

Another way to regain focus is to think about how the foods you are eating at your meal make you feel. If something does not satisfy you or makes you feel strange, you usually know within a few minutes. This will also help you with selecting foods during the next meal.

If you lose focus during your meal and find your thoughts wandering, or you are tempted to multitask, push the food around on your plate for a few seconds. Rate the foods on your plate. Which one would you eat first? Which one is your least favorite? It might seem silly, but little steps like these will keep your focus where it should be.

After your meal is over, you might consider writing about your experience. Keeping a food journal might help you to discover what foods you most enjoy that also do your body good. This step will also help with meal preparation and planning which is a part of mindful eating.

Practical Examples:

Sherry has just begun practicing mindful eating. Like so many people, Sherry notices that she gets distracted easily and her thoughts tend to wander during mealtimes which results in mindless eating. Sherry already knows to put away her electronics and eat at the dining room table to be as free from distraction as possible.

As Sherry sits down for breakfast, she stares at her eggs and toast, but her mind is not on breakfast. She is thinking about the day ahead. Looming deadlines at the office seem overwhelming. Both of her children have sporting events to attend this evening. Her husband, Jack, has to work late, so he will not be able to help Sherry. Before she realizes it, Sherry has almost finished her eggs and half of her toast.

Shaking her head, Sherry is almost tempted to give up the mindful eating concept. Then, she remembers that a co-worker said to simply re-focus. Sherry cuts up her food and remembers to be thankful for what she has. Although she has forgotten some of her meal, she was able to savor the last few bites, and she learned a lesson as well.

Heather is meeting a friend for lunch at her favorite Mexican restaurant. Unfortunately, her friend is running late. Heather begins eating the chips and salsa served to her by the waiter as she waits for her friend. Wondering what could be keeping her friend from being on time, Heather mindlessly shovels the chips and salsa in her mouth.

A few moments later, as she is sipping her tea, Heather notices a heavy feeling in her stomach. She has eaten too much, and Heather's friend joins her at the table. In her mind, Heather is deciding if she should order the main course and make herself sicker by continuing to eat, or if she should just sit with her friend.

These scenarios are filled with imaginary people and situations, but their stories are familiar to you and I because we have been in similar situations. In Sherry's situation, she was able to regain focus, and return to her meal before totally missing the enjoyment of it. On the other hand, Heather overate and made herself sick before she regained focus. For Heather, she cannot get the enjoyment of that meal back, but she can learn from the situation and be prepared for the next time.

I must keep reminding you that mindful eating is not a club with which to beat yourself. It is however, an extremely helpful tool to help you enjoy eating, keep your focus away from food when you are not eating, and to learn from your mistakes.

Chapter Summary

- When eating, eat! Do not multitask. Focus on your food, and if your mind wanders, refocus.
- Multitasking causes failure with mindful eating.
- Mindful eating helps you see all of your reasons for eating, both needful and not needful.
- Multitasking and mindfulness do not mix. The mindful eater focuses on the food while eating. After the meal is finished, the mindful eater turns her focus to another activity.
- You can refocus. If your mind wanders, turn back to your food when eating so you will enjoy your meal and feel satisfied.

In the next chapter, you will learn to consider the source of the food so you can be thankful for what you have and take nothing for granted.

Chapter Six: Consider the Food Source

There are a number of ways to consider the source of your food while eating. Depending upon your food choice, you could think about the process it took to produce the food. You could do this by imagining it on the ground, or being grown in a garden and cared for. Being thankful for the person who cooked and prepared your meal, whether it was a relative, friend, spouse, or restaurant worker, is another way to consider the food source.

A Mindful Reflection

The opposite spectrum of mindful eating is mindless eating. If you have never taken the time to consider where your food comes from, then you still have a bit to learn about eating mindfully. Taking the time for this reflection will cause you to appreciate mealtime more and avoid rushing through it. Thankfulness is a great concept to practice.

Never having been a gardener, I would not know personally the care and patience it takes to take care of a garden, field, or tree where certain foods are planted and later harvested. I am not familiar with the frustrations of a lost crop that one has worked hard to tend. Although I do not have this experience, I have observed those who do.

Taking care of crops is a task that must be attended to on a daily basis. When a seed is planted, it does not spring up out of the ground overnight. Weeks, and often months, of watering and tending, are the order of the days after seeds have been placed in the ground. A great deal of time and effort is given to care for what is planted.

Once a crop is harvested, there are other steps taken to prepare it for the marketplace where you or someone else makes the purchase. I must confess that most of the time I have simply purchased groceries without giving a single thought to the source. My only thought was eating what I had bought. At least, that was the case until I began practicing mindful eating.

Now that I have begun to be grateful for the workers who started at the very beginning with care for what I have, I actually have found that I appreciate and enjoy my food even more. When I reflect in this manner, my eating pace slows. As a result, my habits are much healthier, and I have noticed positive changes in my body and mindset.

Although you might not be able to visit a farm, you have Google. You could search for the process by which some of your favorite foods are prepared. Find out where in our world your food comes from. Reflecting on the process will give you a greater connection and appreciation for what you have so readily available.

Connection Versus Disconnection

When people who are connected with the source of their food are compared with those who are disconnected, you will notice some differences. These are enough to make a difference in the way these people relate to food. Looking at some examples, it is evident that people who are connected this way are more grateful for what they have. Those who are disconnected, as I once was, never give it a second thought which causes them to take meals for granted. Unfortunately, mindless eating is the result.

People who are connected with the source of their food are much more mindful eaters than those who are not. Those disconnected often hurry through meals, rarely taking the time to enjoy them. They miss out on wonderful experiences that keep them from eating mindfully.

Beyond the Packaging

There is more to food than the packaging. Being aware of calories and fat grams is great for information, but it contributes little to mindful eating. Healthy food choices are made by observing how each food affects your body. Dividing foods into good food and bad food categories is not productive. In my experience, it only creates frustration.

Beyond the packaging is a food that went through people who worked hard and long to get it to the supermarket for people to purchase. These people make a living by processing food, but reflection on the process makes it more personal and enjoyable. The mindful eater considers all aspects of what she is eating.

You might be surprised to find that considering the source will cause you to realize that you do not need nearly as much food as you think you do. With this in mind, your groceries will last longer, saving you money in the process. You will also lose weight and be in better health. Mindful eating pays off in more ways than one.

Connection with Culture

Many people enjoy eating foreign cuisine, whether it is Mexican, Italian, or Chinese food as well as a host of foods from other cultures. Eating foods from other cultures provides a new variety. When considering the source, we often learn about the ways other cultures prepare their food. Some ways are similar while others are not.

The same process of mindful eating applies to all types of food from any culture. Think about the similarities and differences in the food from your culture and other cultures. Thankfulness for the food itself and those who brought it to us brings an appreciation that aids us in becoming more mindful eaters.

In most other countries, people do not seem to struggle with overeating as they do in America. That is not to say that there are not certain people in other cultures who do not overeat on a regular basis, but it seems to be the exception and not the rule. On that note, you could observe the eating habits of foreign people. Even in countries like France and Italy where the food is rich, people are still mostly thin. It is my suggestion that these people are mindful eaters. When they are hungry, they eat modest portions while enjoying the food. When they are full, they stop eating and put focus in other places.

While you are learning to become a mindful eater, observe other mindful eaters, whether they are in your culture or not. What are their habits? Do they eat slowly? How much do they eat at one time? What types of food do they choose to eat? What are their activities when they are not eating? If you offered them something to eat right after a meal, would they eat it? These observations will be great examples for you.

Connection with Family

Although holidays can be a time of temptation when it comes to eating, they should be a time when we appreciate our families, particularly those family members who prepare food for us. Family dinners are a great time for mindfulness. If you will use family time as a key to mindful eating, you might find that your eating is more in balance even if there are foods present that you would normally be tempted to overeat.

While spending the time with your family, be thankful for each person, reflecting on the time you have together. Often, as children grow up, families drift apart and only see each other on special occasions. If that is the case with your family, value that time. Cherish the moments that you visit with them. Food is put into its proper perspective, and your relationships with family members become more meaningful.

Thankfulness Verses Greed

Sometimes people overeat for emotional reasons while others overeat out of greed. My use of the word greed is not meant to be degrading. Greed often results from a person going through a time of some sort of deprivation. People who went through a period of time with little food to live on will often demonstrate greed.

There is always hope. A mindset change can be the remedy to the problem. Instead of remembering the times of lack, be thankful for the times of plenty. If you have been through a traumatic situation in which food was used as punishment, seek help. You can be a mindful eater with the right guidance.

One of the ways to overcome a problem with greed, no matter what caused it, is to share food with others. There is something about sharing a meal with someone, or giving, that breaks down barriers between people and creates bonds of friendship. Sharing food with someone else helps you to see their needs more and your needs less which will result in more mindful eating.

Connections Make Food Better

When we share meals with others, we not only connect to the source of the food, but we share connections with people as well. Those are the connections worth maintaining. There are times when we need to eat alone, especially when we first practice mindful eating and are getting used to the basics. Later, there are many times we need to eat with others and share meals with people.

During my first days of mindful eating, a co-worker and I would share snacks and meals when we were hungry. Certain restaurants serve large portions so we took advantage of this situation and shared one meal. We both had plenty to eat. We saved money and formed a friendship.

Try sharing a meal with a friend, family member, or co-worker. Enjoy each other's company as you share it. This experience just might bring mindful eating to a whole new level for you.

Practical Examples

Emily was driving to her mother's home for the Thanksgiving holiday. Usually, she looked forward to this holiday, but this year, she was apprehensive. Her brothers had been arguing so there was tension anytime the family got together.

When she arrived at her mother's home, she noticed that her brothers had already arrived. Entering the house, Emily greeted everyone. Her parents, one brother along with his wife and daughter were present in the living room. The other brother was in the dining room. The tension felt so thick that you could cut it with a knife

Eventually, Emily's mother called everyone into the dining room to eat. Emily, her parents, and the rest of the family watched with tension as the two brothers attempted to be polite to each other. Usually, such a scene would make a person lose her appetite, but Emily found herself hiding in the food to avoid drama. Thankfully, she suddenly realized what she was doing.

Instead of hiding in her plate, Emily engaged her brothers in conversation. At first, it was awkward as each was trying to avoid the other. Finally, the tension seemed to break and the two brothers began talking to each other. It was as if everyone in the room breathed a sigh of relief.

Unfortunately, not all situations have a happy ending like this one, but a mindful eater avoids using food as a shelter from a problem. Instead, a mindful eater is thankful for the food, but even more thankful for the people with which she is eating.

Another example is Brenda who was new to the concept of mindful eating. She seemed to be having some difficulty with the process. It was such a challenge for her to eat slower and take more time with her meals. Not wanting to give up on the process, Brenda began thinking of what she should do.

One evening she went to visit her friend, Lea, who was from Japan. Lea had made Japanese food for dinner. At first, Brenda was a little nervous. She was certain that she would not be able to get through the evening without overeating. She feared such a setback might keep from ever getting past her issues with food.

To her surprise and delight, the evening turned out to be wonderful for Brenda. Lea spent a great deal of time telling her how to make and prepare various Japanese dishes. She also told Brenda about how her life had been in Japan. The conversation had kept everything balanced for Brenda. She enjoyed a delicious meal without overeating because mindful eating played a role in the meal. Brenda did not even think about the mindful eating part of the experience until later.

Any meal can be turned into a good experience that goes beyond the food itself. Be thankful for the all sources of your food. Use all experiences, both positive and negative, as learning tools. By doing this, you will continue to grow as a mindful eater.

Chapter Summary

- Mindfully reflect on the sources of your food such as the original source of planting and harvesting.
- Be thankful for the people who prepare food for you such as family, restaurant workers, and friends.

- Make connections with people and sources of food.
- Be thankful and avoid greed.
- Connections aid the mindful eating process.

In the next chapter, you will learn in detail about emotional eating.

Chapter Seven: Emotional Eating

Throughout this book, the subject of emotional eating has been raised, but in this chapter, it will be discussed in detail. Many women struggle with emotional eating. I know this was true for me. Any extreme emotion that I experienced sent me to the refrigerator. I ate if I was angry. I ate if I was sad. I ate if I was happy. Stuffing or celebrating my emotions always revolved around food, particularly sweets.

If you are an emotional eater, do not give up. Mindful eating will bring the changes you need. You can come to a place where you no longer allow emotions to dictate your eating. Managing our emotions can be a reality for you. If I can grasp this concept, so can you.

Deceitful Emotions

Our human emotions can be tricky. They are fickle as well. One moment, I can feel happy and elated, then, in another moment, I can feel down and depressed. This emotional pendulum swing is part of being a woman to a certain extent, but hormonal imbalances and lack of serotonin can play roles in moods and emotions. If you need to see a physician for these issues, that is understandable, but, whether or not you seek medical help, mindful eating is still right for you.

Many women have stated that emotional highs and lows have been the cause of late-night visits to the kitchen as well as daytime binges. Our minds are tricked into believing that finding just the right food will make us feel better. The trouble is that we never find the right food to soothe our emotions so we keep binging in hopes that we will find it. Such was the case with me, and I have a feeling it is the same with many others. No matter what I ate during these times, it was never enough. Afterward, I was left with an overly full stomach and a load of guilt and shame.

Truth is, when you stuff your emotions with food, you are hungry, just not physically. Often you are hungry for love, affirmation, acceptance, recognition, or even rest. If you perceive that your emotional needs are not being met, without realizing it, you seek to meet those needs with food. It is a common but unhealthy cycle that results in weight gain and other physical issues. Sadly, you still have your emotional issues to deal with too.

It is challenging to overcome emotional eating because, like our minds, emotions are powerful and convincing. They are so powerful that the hunger produced by emotions almost feels like physical hunger. You must exercise mindfulness to tell the difference, but it can be done. All you need to do is decide you are going to take the necessary steps. Your emotions do not have authority over you.

Before the ways to tell if your hunger is physical or emotional are discussed, we will look at some questions that you can answer to determine if you are truly an emotional eater.

- Do you normally eat until you are stuffed?
- Does food make you feel safe?
- Do you feel like food is your friend?
- Do you eat to feel better?
- Do you reward yourself with food?
- Do you eat more when you are stressed?
- Do you celebrate with food?

If you answered "yes" to two or more of these questions, then, you are an emotional eater. In some ways, it was a relief to me when I first realized that I was an emotional eater. It was also a bit disheartening, but at least I knew the truth. You can not fix that which you will not face, so, I was glad to know what the issues were. Mindful eating played a huge role in my path to freedom.

Here is a quick recap of the signs of emotional hunger.

- Emotional hunger comes suddenly rather than gradually.
- Emotional hunger results in mindless eating.
- Emotional hunger craves certain foods and the sooner the food comes, the better.
- Emotional hunger will never be satisfied even if you feel physically stuffed.
- Emotional hunger leads to feelings of guilt and shame.
- Emotional hunger does not come from the stomach.

Being reminded of these factors can help motivate you to look past your emotions and tune in to physical hunger. Dealing with emotions will be discussed later, but for now, we will look at some emotional triggers. If you will observe yourself through mindfulness, you will notice that there are certain situations, places, or even people who cause you to desire to reach out to food for comfort. When you acknowledge this, you can find other strategies to help you deal with your triggers.

The following are some emotional triggers many people experience:

- Stuffing emotions
- Boredom
- Lack of fulfillment
- Social stress
- Other stress
- Habits from childhood

There could even be other triggers so feel free to add more in your journal. I suggest keeping some type of journal through this process. It helps to write experiences down to refer to if you need them later. In addition to the reference, journaling can be a healthy outlet for your emotions successfully keeping you away from the refrigerator.

If you are headed to the kitchen to get something to eat, stop and ask yourself a few questions. Am I physically hungry? Pause and see if you have an empty feeling in your stomach, just below the ribcage. If you are truly hungry, proceed but practice mindful eating. If you are not physically hungry, you do not need to eat, but you need to look further. Ask yourself the following: Am I upset? Am I depressed? Am I stuffing an emotion? Why am I going to food when I am not hungry? As you answer these questions, write the answers in your journal. After a period of time, you will be able to notice the patterns and break them.

If you are lonely or depressed, call a friend, play with your child or a pet, or watch a comical movie or television show. If you are anxious, take a walk or squeeze a stress ball. If you are tired, rest by taking a bath, wrapping yourself up in a warm blanket, or taking a nap. If you are bored, read a book, watch a movie, or engage in an activity that you enjoy that does not require eating. If you think of other ways to fulfill emotional needs, feel free to try those. Be sure you write those ideas down for future reference.

In my own experience, I have found that if I do not get enough sleep, my emotions tend to swing to the extreme side. Often, our struggles with depression, anger, and other difficult emotions are the result of a lack of sleep. It is important that you get at least seven hours of sleep per night.

Deal with Your Emotions

If your negative emotions are not dealt with in some way, you will continue on in an emotional eating frenzy. Even your positive emotions must have a creative outlet. Find other ways to celebrate a milestone or event besides eating. Going bowling or to see a movie is a celebration as well. Stay away from the popcorn unless you have saved room for it.

Denying that your emotions are an issue is not healthy, and, neither is ignoring your emotions. Ignoring a problem does not make it non-existent. It is fine to acknowledge those emotions. You can say, "I feel angry right now." You can say, "I am depressed today." Be honest about your emotions, but do not let them dictate you by going on a binge or lashing out at someone.

If your emotions are extremely out of control, seeing a counselor might be helpful. Not everyone who has emotional issues needs a counselor or therapy, but there is certainly nothing wrong with going for that type of help if it is needed. Whatever is needed to get you healthier is exactly what should be done if possible.

In some societies, people have not been taught to deal with what is difficult or challenging. While this might seem pleasant, it is hardly helpful. Many children and adults have not been taught to allow themselves to feel and work through the unpleasant emotions.

If you are angry, acknowledge the anger. Feel it, but do not let it spin out of control. If you are sad, go through the experience, but do not stay there. If you are depressed, allow yourself to feel the emotion, then, deal with it. Is there a legitimate reason to feel depressed such as a loss or major change in life? If not, then it could be an issue that requires medical help. Mindfulness does not encourage denying the emotion. You are encouraged to face it and deal with it.

Another emotional eating factor that has not been discussed is body hate. If you hate your body, you will not make permanent changes that are needed. Some people claim that their hatred of their bodies will change when they reach a desired weight goal. I can tell you that will not be the case because I have seen other people reach their goal weight after a long struggle, yet, still hate their bodies. Hating your body is a process that needs to be dealt with. I am not sure I can cover that in this book except to tell you that you must look at the things your body can do such as walking, running, seeing, hearing, etc. Be thankful for those functions and remember that you could not do those things without your body. Seeing a counselor or therapist might be helpful in this case as well.

Earlier, emotional triggers were discussed. Knowing your emotional triggers is important because you can still practice mindful eating, but it would be beneficial to deal with some of the sources of negative emotions if possible. For example, if you are angry over something that happened in your childhood, you must deal with the source of that problem.

If you are still harboring anger over a past incident that can not be made right, you have to find a way to let that go. You must say, "This happened. It should not have happened. It is not fair, but there is nothing I can do about it. I do not want this to follow me the rest of my life so I am choosing to move on." You might not be cured right away, but you are taking steps in the right direction. It might be necessary to go for counseling if you are unable to recover from emotional wounds from the past.

If you are stressed out, look at the cause of the stress. If something can be eliminated from your life, then remove it. If it is a situation that you are unable to walk away from, then you must have a strategy to deal with the situation. Counselors are a good source for those types of strategies. In the meantime, you can still practice mindful eating so that the issue does not spill over into your eating habits any more than it already has.

In the Meantime

Some negative emotions take time to deal with, especially if they stem from a traumatic experience. While you are in the process of coping, there are some steps you can take to make mindful eating successful for you. If there is a food from which you are unable to stop yourself from overeating, it might be necessary to remove that item from your home. You might have to avoid eating that food for a time until you are able to bring issues under control.

For example, if you binge on cookies or cakes, and you can not stop yourself, remove cookies and cakes from your home, and do not bring them back into your home until you know you are able to control yourself. This is only meant to be a temporary measure. Eventually, you should be able to deal with having that food back in the house again.

Keep practicing mindful eating even when your emotions seem to spin out of control. Mindful eating will provide some stability for you. When your emotions are unstable, mindful eating will keep your eating habits stable. You might have to work harder than some people would who do not have your struggles, but the work will be worth it when you have your eating under control and your weight begins to drop.

It is important to be completely aware of your emotional triggers. If not, you will be swept into an eating binge before you know it. When you are facing the temptation to go to food because you have been triggered emotionally, stop what you are doing. Put off eating for at least five minutes. Go outside if you need to. Call a friend. Take a walk. Find something that you normally enjoy doing. If you can keep yourself occupied for a while, your chances are better of avoiding a binge.

If you catch yourself in the middle of a binge, stop immediately. Even if you have already eaten much more than you should have, stop! Give yourself credit for stopping before you completed the binge. Although it might not seem to be a victory, you have made a step in the right direction. Get away from the source of temptation. Get away from the food. Find something creative and constructive to occupy you.

According to medical experts in the area of emotional eating, boredom is one of the triggers to avoid at all costs. Keep yourself occupied either with work or activities you enjoy while in between meals. When you find yourself tempted to eat out of boredom, focus on an activity such as a game or a tv show.

Even if you are physically hungry and still feel some negative emotions, it is a good idea to calm those emotions before eating. If not, it will be difficult to eat mindfully. I am not suggesting that you would be completely unable to eat mindfully when your emotions are somewhat high, but I know it makes the process less complicated. I want you to be successful.

Have someone to whom you can be accountable. When your emotions are deceiving you, having someone who can be objective will be extremely helpful. Give this person permission to hold you accountable and talk you through an emotional situation. Sometimes we need the help of others, and there should be no shame in seeking that help. There are a number of online support groups for people who are learning to eat mindfully.

High levels of cortisol are released into your body during times of stress which produce the "fight or flight response". This will cause you to feel as if you need to eat even if you are not hungry. Practice breathing techniques if you are anxious, take a walk, or do some type of exercise to relieve stress.

If you are going to be in a tempting situation such as an evening out with friends at your favorite restaurant, or a celebration dinner at your job, have a strategy. Social situations often bring anxiety to emotional eaters. Being prepared is a major part of the battle. If you are going to a restaurant, plan ahead what you are going to order and stick to it. Ask for a go-box and only eat half of your entree. If necessary, put the other half in the go-box before you begin eating. If you are going to a celebration dinner on your job or at a family member's home, serve yourself on a small plate, and do not go back for seconds.

These techniques might sound a bit extreme, but sometimes it takes extra steps that might not be convenient for you to get on the right track. In the long run, you will be glad you took the trouble. The end is definitely worth the means.

Chapter Summary

- Emotions are deceitful.
- Emotional hunger is sudden, not gradual.
- Emotional hunger brings cravings.
- Emotional hunger is never satisfied.
- When you are getting ready to eat, ask yourself why you are eating.
- Use a journal to keep track of emotions and progress.
- Do not deny or suppress your emotions.
- Deal with your emotions.
- When anxious, practice breathing techniques.
- Get accountability.

If you are enjoying this book book so far, I would appreciate it so much if you would go to Amazon and leave a short review.

In the next chapter, you will learn how to change your thinking.

Chapter Eight: You Can Change Your Thinking

Everyone knows that the mind is powerful. It has the capability to convince us that something is real when it is false. Like our emotions, the mind can often deceive us. We might feel powerless under our mind's control, but the fact is we can change the way we think. I know this is true for me. At one time, most of my thoughts about food were entirely negative. I was obsessed with every bite in my mouth. Either I felt I could not survive without that one bite, or, I was convinced that every bite I took was causing me to gain more weight. Obsession is never healthy. If I was able to change my thinking about food and the way I eat, you can do the same.

What Are You Thinking?

Your thoughts can go in so many random directions that it is important to stop and assess your thoughts. Are your thoughts productive or destructive? Will the thought pattern you are in help you to live your life in a better way, or will it cause you to become negative and self-destructive? If your thoughts are not going in a positive pattern, it is time to break the pattern. Why is that so important? You will eventually act upon that which you are thinking. Thoughts eventually become actions.

Right now, you might be wondering how to change your thoughts. I will tell you that it does take time and work, but it is completely doable. First, assess your thoughts to see what your mind is dwelling upon. You would be surprised at how often our minds go in a negative direction, and we do not catch it.

I will use myself as an example. What if I thought nothing but negative thoughts about a friend of mine? There could have been an incident in which I became frustrated with her, but I did not deal with it. Not having let it go, everything my friend does will irritate me. The irritation will keep festering until I eventually lash out at her. The incident does not even have to be serious to cause frustration and irritation, but it is situations such as these in which tension builds that cause emotional outbursts and emotional eating.

There are a few steps I could take to prevent this. When I first became irritated with my friend, I should have decided in my mind if the situation was worth staying irritated over. If so, I needed to speak to my friend about it. If not, I needed to let it go by refusing to dwell on it. Yes, you can refuse to dwell on certain thoughts. You have to replace it with another way of thinking. When my thoughts tried to return to what irritated me with my friend, I could choose to think about the good things she has done. After that, I could choose to think about something else entirely.

If my thoughts about eating are negative and non-productive, I can change those. When I am beginning to dwell on what I am going to have for lunch, even though it has already been planned, I am allowing the concept of food to dominate my thinking. I have to break that pattern by reminding myself that it is not lunch time yet so I should not need to have my mind on food, especially since I have already planned the meal. After the reminder to myself, it is important that I begin to replace that thinking with another thinking pattern. I need to focus on the task or activity on which I am currently working, or, I need to think about another enjoyable activity that I love to do.

Banish the Thought

Any negative or non-productive thoughts I have about food and eating have to be pushed away and replaced with something better. For example, if I am thinking about how horribly I am doing at mindful eating and how much I have failed at the process, I am not going to do better. Instead, I need to tell myself that it is great that I have started eating mindfully. I was not even doing that before. I should also remind myself that I am excited about ways I can improve rather than believing that it will never get better.

I am going to use Beth again as an example. Beth has been struggling with mindful eating. She will stay focused for a while then drift back into mindless eating. She chides herself that she needs to do better, but when she does not get better, she begins thinking about what a hopeless mess she believes she is. Although that might seem like a humble undertaking, it is very self-destructive. Instead of berating herself, Beth should remind herself that just a few months prior to now she did not even know what mindful eating was. Now, she is taking steps to eat better. Learning can be an enjoyable experience so Beth should be excited to learn about the ways she can do better with mindful eating. Do you see the difference? The more positive approach is much more effective.

When you banish a thought, so to speak, you will not be able to totally be free from it until you find something with which to replace it. To stop negative thinking is not enough, the thoughts have to be replaced with something better. The quicker you catch the negativity and replace it with something more positive, the easier the process is.

Total Replacement

It is important to remember not to chide yourself for having negative thoughts. Simply catch it and change the pattern. When replacing a negative or destructive thought, it is essential to take the thought not only in a different direction but also to leave no room for your mind to turn and go back to the old way of thinking. This type of change comes neither quickly nor easily, but it can be done.

When a car battery is being replaced, the entire battery is removed. The mechanic would not leave pieces of the old battery and try attaching it to the new battery. It would be ridiculous to even try it. Like the mechanic, you do not need to leave even a hint of your negative thinking concerning food behind. If so, it will keep the new way of thinking from becoming effective. A complete change is necessary.

To change your thoughts about mindful eating, do not entertain the thoughts that say, "You can't do this." Resist and banish the thoughts that say, "This is too hard. It will never work." Instead, say, "I can do this." Remind yourself that it might be hard, but it can be done. It will work if you are consistent. At first, you will have to repeat this process many times. Eventually, it becomes easier.

In order to change negative or destructive thought patterns, you must first be aware of it. As stated before, you must assess your thinking. If needed, write down some of your observed thought patterns. While taking part in this process, avoid having a judgmental attitude toward yourself. Berating yourself does nothing to solve the problem.

After becoming aware, it is important to recognize when you have actually started into a negative thought process. It could be rather challenging, but try interrupting your thoughts when you realize that your thoughts are going in the wrong direction. Sometimes, just speaking out loud interrupts a thought pattern. It is important to switch gears as quickly as possible so when you realize what is happening, take immediate action.

Once you begin changing the pattern, you can acknowledge your thought pattern by reminding yourself that thinking negatively does nothing to make the situation better. Begin replacing the pattern with a more positive one. For example, you might start thinking something like this: "Mindful eating is a waste of time, and it is too much work." If you continue this pattern, you will talk yourself right out of mindful eating. Now, you must interrupt that thought. If necessary, speak out loud, or focus on something that someone is saying by listening to the radio, or watching a program on television. After a moment, remind yourself of the following: "Mindful eating might seem like hard work and a waste of time because it does require a little extra time, but it is going to be worth it when I develop new eating habits and feel better." You might have to repeat this process over and over for a while because changing your thinking does take time.

Distorted Thinking Patterns

Distortions are simply ways our minds convince us that something is true when it is not. Awareness of these patterns will keep you on guard so that when your thoughts attempt to take on these patterns, you will stop it before it gets started. Look at the following distortions and see if you recognize them.

- Filtering: Your mind will take negative details and filter out the positive ones from a situation.
- Black and White Thinking: There are no gray areas or middle ground with this pattern. It is one extreme or the other. For example, I am either a complete success or a complete failure.
- Overgeneralization: This type of thinking comes to a general conclusion based on only one piece of evidence. If you have one unpleasant day or event, you just assume that every other day or event will be the same way.

- Jumping to Conclusions: When engaged in this type of thinking you will assume you know exactly how someone feels about you or a situation. You never seek to determine if you are correct. It never occurs to you that you could be wrong.
- Catastrophizing: If you are engaged in this pattern, you will make something significant out of what is insignificant. No matter what, you are sure disaster will strike. With this type of thinking, you can also minimize events by taking something significant and making it seem of no importance.

If you recognize any or all of these patterns in yourself, do not despair. You are not hopeless. If you recognize these patterns, it is a sign that you are ready to take action to change.

Maintain Your Mindfulness

Once you have developed a new habit of thinking more positive and productive thoughts, maintenance is essential. If done properly, maintenance will not be as difficult and challenging as changing the negative thought pattern. When you are in the habit of thinking productively, it will be easier to recognize when a thought comes that does not fit the pattern. This will be a lifetime process, but it will not be difficult if you have taken the time to break the destructive patterns.

In order to maintain good thought patterns, avoid a comfort zone. It is possible that a comfort zone brought you to negative thinking. If not, then it is possible to develop a comfort zone in which you feel safe. The fact is that you are not truly safe. You are setting yourself up to return to destructive thinking. Do activities in small steps that are outside of what you normally do. This will make you slowly come out of your comfort zone without the process being frightening. Engaging in activities that make you uncomfortable is one of the best ways to come out of any comfort zone you have developed. The zone feels comfortable, but it is not helping you to make the changes needed.

Although you are thinking more mindfully, avoid overthinking. This will lead you back to negative and destructive thought patterns. Mindfulness means living in the present. Avoid living too much in the past or future. Learn from the past, make some plans for the future, but live in the present.

Do not allow yourself a long time to make food choices. Think over your options quickly but efficiently, then, make a choice. Taking too long to choose what you are going to eat will frustrate you causing you to miss the entire point of the mindful eating process. Once again, being mindful is not the same as overthinking.

If you are maintaining mindful eating processes, your actions will reflect the results. From time to time, assess your actions as well as your thoughts. If you are not overeating, and you are enjoying your meals, you are maintaining the ground you have gained. If you have lost weight, or you are still losing weight, you are maintaining mindful eating processes.

Should you notice that you are slowly slipping back into old habits, it's time to evaluate your thinking again. Have you been waiting until you are truly hungry to eat? Are you eating slowly and focusing on the food while eating? Do you avoid dwelling on thoughts of food when you are not eating unless it is to plan a meal for later? What types of thoughts are you entertaining? Answering these questions will help you to determine if adjustments need to be made. The quicker you catch negative thinking patterns trying to slip back in, the quicker you can resolve the issue before you have a total setback.

Remember that it was the right patterns of thought that changed your life. Change, positive or negative, begins with your thinking. Be mindful of your thought patterns to maintain the positive change you have seen.

Practical Examples

Christina has faced a great deal of adverse circumstances in her life. She was abandoned by her parents as a child, but she was later adopted by a loving family who did everything they could to make her life pleasant. Although her adopted family always showed her love, Christina dwelled on the fact that she was abandoned by her biological parents.

After graduating from High School, Christina married the first man who showed interest in her. She was grateful to find someone because she believed that she was not worth loving. As the years went by, Christina's negativity toward herself and others began affecting her current marriage. Rather than seek to solve the problem, Christina began comforting herself by emotional eating.

Eventually, Christina and her husband divorced. They never had any children. Christina continued to pursue her downward spiral of emotional eating and avoiding relationships. She knows that something must change, but she is not sure what, if anything, can be done.

So many people come from backgrounds similar to Christina. Although it is tragic to be abandoned by one's biological parents, Christina was given a loving family. Rather than enjoy what she was given, she focused on what she had lost. This negative pattern of thinking affected her marriage and led to her seeking food for comfort.

Had Christina recognized her destructive thinking patterns, she could have taken steps to change them. In turn, she would have enjoyed her relationship with her adopted family. Perhaps her marriage would have lasted. When she began turning to emotional eating, she needed to practice mindful eating which could have helped her come to the realization of where destructive thought patterns lead.

Karen is married and has three children. Her husband has a good job, but he is seldom home. Karen works part-time at a local bank. During the evenings, she is usually taking her children to sporting events and other school events.

By the time she works, keeps her house clean, cooks, does laundry, and takes her children to their events, Karen feels exhausted and taken for granted. Rather than speak to her husband or a friend about how she is feeling, Karen begins indulging in late night snacks. These snacks eventually become episodes of binging.

Eventually, Karen begins gaining weight which causes her to go to a larger size in clothes. Realizing she has to do something, Karen begins to practice mindful eating, a technique she heard about from her sister. At first, Karen has some success and loses weight. However, Karen does not deal with negative thought patterns which eventually causes her to slip back into old habits.

Like many other women, Karen is a busy mom. Karen has a choice. She can continue living the way she is, but try to find a way to cope. She can ask for help from her husband or a family member. Her children are both old enough to help out around the house so she could delegate some duties. When it comes to her eating, Karen could remind herself that food is not solving her problems. Realizing that she is slipping back into old habits, Karen has the chance to stop, assess her thinking, and make the adjustments that are necessary to get her eating habits under control.

When you find yourself slipping back into old habits and patterns of thinking. Stop! Do not keep going on that way. You, like Karen, have the opportunity to adjust your thinking and return to mindful eating. It might take a bit of effort, but it is much better than going back into a complete setback.

Chapter Summary

- Determine where your thoughts are going.
- Banish thoughts that are not productive.
- Replace an old pattern of thinking with a new one.
- Recognize distorted thinking.
- Maintain your mindfulness by making adjustments in your thinking when needed.

In the next chapter, you will learn more about how to enjoy eating without guilt.

Chapter Nine: Enjoy Eating When It's Time to Eat

Guilt-free eating should be a given when you sit down for your meals. Sadly, for people who have struggled with food issues, that is not the case. Guilt has been ingrained so deeply in the souls of some people that it will take some great effort and pain to be free from it. Eating is an activity that is meant to be enjoyed. It is not to be abused, but after you have taken all precautions, you do not have to feel guilty and ashamed because you enjoy eating.

No More Guilt!

Now that you are learning to enjoy a variety of foods, give yourself permission to be free from guilt. If guilt has been your lifelong companion, your unwanted friend will not leave immediately; however, do not give up. Keep pushing guilt to the door of your mind and bid him goodbye!

Guilt has a cousin named Shame. If you have struggled with your weight and disordered eating for too long, they both like to show up and attempt to rob you of your peace and joy. You are now a mindful eater, so, you do not have to put up with the negative company, and that includes your emotions. Acknowledge them but refuse them power. They do not get to decide how you experience eating. You are in charge of your feelings.

Pay Attention to Your Thought Patterns

When you are eating, pay attention to your thoughts. They have a tendency to drift in the wrong direction causing you to forget about mindful eating. You are in charge now, so, take control. Turn the attention back to eating and enjoy every taste, every bite. Chew slowly and really taste your food. The more you practice this part of mindful eating, the better you will be at it. You might be surprised to find that it will not take much food to satisfy you. For a long time, you have not truly enjoyed eating because you have rushed. Now, by slowing down, you will be able to have joy in your experience, and you will be more aware of your thought pattern.

When you are not eating, still pay attention to your thoughts. Our minds often want to wander to food unnecessarily. You do not need to dwell on the subjects food and eating when you are not hungry. Continue finding activities and tasks to occupy your mind. Stay out of the kitchen if you do not have a reason to be there.

Tips to Enjoy Guilt-Free Eating

First, you should eat for pleasure. There is nothing wrong with completely enjoying a meal if you are truly hungry. Eliminate thoughts of good foods and bad foods. Some foods are more beneficial than others, but you can enjoy all foods in moderate amounts. Some medical experts say that eating for pleasure is as good for your body as eating for nutrition. The reason for this is because our brain and body react a certain way to pleasurable eating that is good for the metabolism.

If you are stressed out while you are eating, even if you like the food, your body is responding to this stress by partially shutting down the digestive system. Stress affects so much of your health and well being. If your body remains in this state, your body releases extra cortisol which will result in more stored fat.

Although treats should not be eaten on a regular basis, the concept of good food versus bad food needs to be forgotten. This type of thinking puts you in guilt mode when you eat causing you to obsess over every bite you put in your mouth. Obsession in any form or fashion is not a part of mindful eating. It might seem that you are being carefully considerate, but obsession brings negative consequences with it. Overthinking is not productive.

Secondly, eating with family and friends brings back the joy of eating. Not only is this a pleasurable bonding time for you and your family, but it is also a great time to contribute to positive experiences with food for your children and the children in your family. Tell them about family recipes, and involve them in the preparation. The more healthy and positive experiences children have with food, the less likely they will be to develop disordered eating.

Next, have a balanced meal when possible. Try choosing nutrients from as many food groups as possible. Having a balance of proteins, carbohydrates, and fats brings a balance and can prevent you from having the desire to binge later.

Fourth, moderation is the key. Too much or too little of any food group will open you up to feel some type of deprivation later. Instead of eating a large portion of meat, choose to eat about one-half to three-fourths of it. Instead of a large baked potato, have a smaller one. These minor changes can make a difference in your weight and eating satisfaction.

Next, do not be afraid to try something different. Variety prevents boredom. Having a variety of food in your diet keeps your mind from wandering when you are eating. When you constantly eat the same foods at every meal, you become bored and begin to eat mindlessly.

When you are eating, compare foods. Doing this will give you a better idea of varying textures and tastes that make your eating experience much more interesting. You will also find yourself eating slower which is always a plus.

While all foods are fine for you to eat (unless you are diabetic), save your favorite foods for certain times or occasions. Practicing this step will keep your favorite foods from becoming mundane. You want to keep your experience positive.

Practice pausing. Before eating, pause to look at the food on your plate. Observe the various colors and shapes of your food. Take in the aroma. Pause between bites, putting your utensils down, and taking a sip of water or another beverage. If you notice that you are eating without tasting, pause and look at the food again.

Enjoy every bite or spoonful. Do not put more food into your mouth until you have tasted the bite you currently have. Unless you are eating soup, use a small spoon. Enjoying every bite will take time to acquire since you are used to fast-paced eating, but you can get there with time and practice.

I realize that this point will sound redundant, but sit down when you are eating. Throughout this book, I have stressed the point of sitting. The reason for this is because sitting is one way to relax. If you are not relaxed, you will not eat mindfully. If your body is tense, signals of stress are sent to the brain. Your body will be tricked into thinking that it is time for defenses to go up and to give you a "fight or flight" response. This is the opposite of the effect you want while eating mindfully.

Some nutrition experts have suggested that a variety of colors on your plate is pleasing to the eye. With this in mind, people are more likely to enjoy the eating experience more with a colorful plate. Although this might not be totally necessary, variety is always good, and it certainly will not make matters worse to try more color.

A Reminder: Turn Off Distraction

Turning off your cell phone, computer, television, or any other electronic device is a must. I know it has been mentioned several times in this book, but it is a crucial point. Total attention to your food during meals is what prevents unreasonable cravings and a desire to binge later. At any rate, time away from electronics has a number of other benefits along with helping your eating experience to become more mindful.

Experts claim that cell phones are a distraction even when they are not on. Just having them in the room with you is an automatic cue for you to give thought as to whom you might need to text, or, the email to which you feel you must respond. Studies have shown that people's work performance is impaired by the overuse of cell phones. Since that is the case, your mealtime can be impaired as well. Because of these factors, it would be best not only to have your phone turned off but to have it out of the room as well. Put it somewhere in which you will have to be inconvenienced to get it.

Another suggestion given by nutrition experts is to play soft music while eating. They claim that it is relaxing and will enhance your dining mood as well as keep you away from electronic devices. Since enjoyment of meals is the goal, playing soft music if you enjoy it would be a plus.

Comfort Food: Yay or Nay

Foods that we associate with good memories are often called comfort food. If your mother made a certain type of cake for you when you were a child, the memory of that cake brings you comfort. You might seek out cake when you are stressed as a way to comfort yourself. Of course, this not only applies to cake. It could be any foods that bring a good memory.

Comfort foods are often high in sugar or sodium. If eaten in moderation on certain occasions, these foods would be fine. The concern is that comfort foods have often been abused due to emotional eating issues. Although we want to lose the good food versus bad food mentality, foods with which you have had binging issues should be approached with caution.

These types of foods turn on what is known as the brain's reward system. As a result, your mood will be happy, unpleasant feelings will be reduced, and tension lessened. Who would not want to eat these foods? If you practice mindful eating, these foods would be fine. On the other hand, if you find yourself tempted to binge, it might be a good idea to stay away from it. Just make caution the order of the day.

Why Comfort Foods Comfort

Comfort foods feel good. Food that is loaded with sugar, sodium, or fat has been known to activate the brain's reward system. Pleasant feelings are increased while tension is decreased. These foods activate the same portions of the brain that are active with drug addiction.

Without realizing it, people use comfort food to self-medicate. Emotional eaters are highly likely to use food for this purpose. When depressed, people are most frequently drawn to fattening foods. The problem is that the moods will eventually come back down, almost like a crash. Mindful eating is encouraged to get past emotional eating.

Certain foods are associated with family members and social gatherings. When an emotional eater is lonely or depressed, she tends to crave these foods. The power is in the association. People who have positive relationships with family are very likely to turn to these foods when experiencing negative emotions.

There is a strong association with certain aromas and pleasant past memories. When people are drawn to these foods for this reason, it is known as nostalgic eating. Simply another aspect of emotional eating, memories draw you to indulge in these foods. If you are truly hungry, then there is no harm, but if you are overindulging, it can cause negative effects.

Some emotional eaters are drawn to special occasion eating. The problem is that they want the occasions to be frequent. It is as if they are caught between celebration mode and mindful eating mode. They want the best of both worlds, but, sooner or later, a choice must be made.

Mindful eating can bring all of these types of emotional eating types back into perspective. Anytime you eat, remember to ask yourself if you are truly hungry. If not, simply wait. Occupy your mind with a task or activity as has been discussed in previous chapters. If you are hungry, proceed, but be mindful of the choices you make. Choose a balanced variety of that which will truly sustain you. Treats are fine from time to time, but they should not be an everyday occurrence. There are plenty of choices in sustaining foods that should satisfy your taste buds.

Reminders About Slowing Down

People often get irritated with those who eat slowly, but if you truly take a look, the slow eaters are usually the ones who are slim. When we eat too rapidly, we can overeat before the stomach has a chance to signal the brain that it is full. Eating slowly increases the pleasure in eating. This sounds simple enough, but if you are in the habit of eating fast, it might not be so simple.

When you are stressed, experts have suggested taking a few ten to fifteen-minute mini-breaks. These breaks will relieve stress which will help you slow down when you eat. If you still have difficulty slowing down when eating, remember to put your utensil down between bites as well as sip water or another beverage between bites. Pause for a moment to see if you are approaching satisfaction.

Eating slowly has a more calming effect on your body. When you eat too fast, your digestive system is put under stress. Poor digestion will eventually lead to other stomach issues. The reason for this is because the GI tract is not prepared to deal with food that has not been chewed properly.

A study was conducted among a group of women. When these women would eat rapidly, they consumed around six hundred fifty calories in nine minutes. When they would eat slowly, they consumed about five hundred eighty calories in twenty-nine minutes. That is a significant difference. Slower eating will result in you eating less food plus provide a number of other benefits.

Another study among women demonstrated that women who eat slowly remained sustained for a longer period of time. The women who ate rapidly felt hungry a short time after eating. A greater food consumption actually satisfied these women less. Faster is not better.

These studies and reminders should motivate us to slow down. If putting the utensils down and sipping between bites does not help, remember to chew more slowly and really savor the food. You could also excuse yourself from the table for a minute or two which would give you time to adjust so you could return and eat slower.

Additional Pointers to Enjoy Eating

The reason slow eating has been stressed so strongly in this book is that part of mindful eating is to enjoy eating. If you do not enjoy eating, you will feel deprived later and be tempted to binge. You want all the pleasure and benefits you can get from eating. Allowing yourself the enjoyment will help with cravings later.

You are free to enjoy eating without guilt. Some people have abuse in their pasts where food is concerned. As a result, they often feel guilty for every bite they put in their mouths. Mindful eating has no guilt. When practicing mindful eating, you will begin to make choices that are best for you and your body. Do not allow anyone to make you feel guilty. If you were abused as a child or at some point in your life, and food was withheld from you, or you were forced to eat, counseling might be necessary.

Sometimes eating by yourself is good, particularly when you first begin practicing mindful eating. Other times, having someone to eat with you, whether it is friends, family, or a coworker is great for mindful eating. Not only are you enjoying a pleasant eating experience, but you are bonding socially.

It is important that you select foods that you enjoy eating. You might have to broaden your horizons and be willing to try foods you have not thought of before. Trying different foods is a way to have more of a variety instead of eating the same foods meal after meal which will cause you to become tired of these foods. This can cause you issues with your eating. Just feel free to experiment, but choose foods you enjoy. Your mindfulness will guide you into great decision making where food is concerned.

Practical Examples

Betty and Anna are the best of friends. They usually go everywhere together. When you see one, you see the other.

Betty is thin and has rarely had any issues with her weight. Whenever she did gain a few pounds, she seemed to have no problems reducing her food intake and losing weight. She always eats slowly and enjoys her food. Betty does not eat unless she is hungry. Usually, she does not overeat. If she does have a time in which she overindulges, Betty waits until she is certain that she is truly hungry before eating again.

Anna, on the other hand, has always struggled to keep her weight down. At times, Anna's weight is like a pendulum swing. It goes back and forth and is not stable. Anna is a fast eater and usually eats nearly twice what Betty does. As a matter of fact, Anna gets a bit frustrated with Betty for eating so slowly. Anna often seeks comfort foods and consumes them in large amounts. When Anna is not eating, she is usually thinking about food. She talks about food incessantly as well.

Rather than become frustrated at Betty, perhaps Anna could learn to eat slower as Betty does. Anna would certainly enjoy her food which would result in less talking and thinking about food in between meals. Because Anna eats so quickly, she is not satisfied which leads to obsessive thinking and often binging.

Once Anna begins eating slower, she will be able to determine true hunger and fullness. She could find some activity to occupy her in between meals as well. Anna also needs to practice mindfulness so she realizes when she physically hungry. These small changes will gradually help Anna to be a great mindful eater.

Cathy has always had disordered eating. As a child, food was withheld from her as punishment. Now, as an adult, Cathy binges on various foods, and she eats extremely fast. Cathy knows her habits are not healthy, and she cries herself to sleep most nights. She truly wants to make a change, but Cathy is not certain of the steps she should take.

One day, a friend mentions that she has started practicing mindful eating. Cathy begins to ask questions about the process. The more Cathy talks to her friend, the more she believes mindful eating is right for her. Cathy makes a decision to begin mindful eating.

She starts slowly, practicing mindful eating for one meal per day. Soon, she begins practicing mindful eating at every meal. After a period of time, Cathy notices that her clothes fit more loosely. For the first time in her life, Cathy feels hopeful. With determination and mindfulness, Cathy knows she will get on track and develop better eating habits.

Situations like Cathy's are far too common. Mindful eating is right for Cathy, but accountability with her friend would benefit her immensely. It will take time for Cathy to work through the emotional pain, but she can do it. She is on the right track, and so are you.

Chapter Summary

- Learn to eat guilt-free.
- There is no shame in enjoying food.
- Pay attention to thought patterns.
- Eat for pleasure.

- Eat for sustenance.
- Stress affects eating pleasure.
- Obsession is not a part of mindful eating.
- Try different foods.
- Eat what you enjoy.
- Approach comfort foods with caution.
- Practice pausing.
- Enjoy every bite.
- Sit, sit, sit.
- Turn off distractions.
- Slow down when eating.

In the next and final chapter, you will be reminded that you are a mindful eater, and you will be encouraged and motivated to keep going.

Chapter Ten: You Are a Mindful Eater

In this final chapter, I hope to impart some encouragement and motivation to you. For the last nine chapters, you have been given a great deal of information that you will not necessarily absorb the first time you go through this book. A successful process such as mindful eating takes time to totally comprehend. There are so many learning experiences along the way, but it is the experiences that will bring permanent change to your health.

Throughout your mindful eating experience, you will probably need to refer to various portions of this book repeatedly. This book has been entitled *The Mindful Eating Bible* because it is meant to be used as a reference as well as reading material. When you need to review certain techniques, or simply need motivation, it is my hope that you will use this book over and over again.

You Are Mindful

You might not feel mindful. Perhaps you do not feel the least bit successful, but the fact is, you must have confidence in yourself. People have told you that you can not overcome the obstacles in your life. Do not listen! There will not only be your own thoughts with which to contend, but you will also have to learn to tune out the negative voices of others. You can do well with this process. You can eat mindfully. You can allow mindfulness to change other areas of your life as well.

When you feel discouraged, find someone who is positive to motivate you to keep going. Fill your life with positive influences. Avoid negative people, and do not become a negative person. Negativity will spill over into every part of your life, including your eating. For some, it is negativity that brought them to the place they are trying to escape. Negativity will not keep you mindful.

Reminder: Listen to Your Body

If you will listen to your body, you will find that you receive signals for most needs. When you are hungry, you will have an empty, burning sensation right below the ribcage. Sometimes this sensation will be accompanied by a growl. The true need for food will not rise from your emotions.

When you need to stop eating, you will feel the food in your stomach, but you will not be stuffed. If you continue to eat beyond this point, you will overeat. You will know when you have overeaten because you will feel stuffed. You might even have some stomach pain or discomfort.

When you need something to drink, you will get a signal from your body. Most likely, your mouth and throat will feel dry. Often, people think they are hungry when they are truly thirsty. Always assess yourself to see if you are thirsty before you eat if you are not certain of the signals you are receiving.

Your body will let you know when you need to rest. Usually, you will be tired or sleepy. Other times you might become irritable or cross with others if you have not had enough sleep. Another sign of lack of sleep is the inability to concentrate. Lack of rest can contribute to overeating so get your sleep! The body needs at least seven hours of sleep each night.

When you are in pain, cold, or hot, your body gives you signals. Your body was designed to send signals to the brain when you are in need of something, or if there is a problem that needs to be addressed. If you will listen to your physical body rather than your emotions, you will be able to improve mindful eating practices.

Reminder: The Hunger Scale

You can use the hunger scale in Chapter One to rate your hunger. Mostly, you should be somewhere between two to five on the scale. If you fall below two, you will become ravenous which makes you at risk for overeating and eating too rapidly. If you go beyond five, you are eating more than you need.

It is amazing to realize that it only takes small amounts of food to satisfy us. We probably do not need one-half to three-fourths of the food we have been accustomed to eating. When you first begin mindful eating, try cutting your portions back by half. After that, you can make adjustments as needed.

Have a Plan

Always have a plan of action to rely upon if you are tempted to eat outside of the boundaries of hunger and fullness. Have activities available or work to do that will keep your mind occupied when you should not be dwelling on food. Using a journal to document your progress is helpful. The journal can also be used for reminders such as follows:

"I do not need to eat if I am not hungry."

"I can always eat later."

If you think of others, write those in your journal or on some index cards.

Finding Fullness

Remember that your stomach is only the size of a loosely clenched fist. Although you do not have to measure every bite of food you eat by your fist, this will serve as a great reminder that it does not take so much food to satisfy. Stop between bites to make sure you are not approaching the point of enough as it takes the stomach a few minutes to signal to the brain that you are full.

If you overeat, there is no need to condemn yourself. Simply remember the feeling of being overly full for the next eating experience. Wait for physical hunger before eating again. Observing our mistakes rather than beating ourselves up will help us grow in our mindful eating experience.

Reminder: Physical and Emotional Hunger

Emotional hunger can seem overwhelming. It can be extremely convincing so it is important to review the signs of physical and emotional hunger.

Emotional hunger comes on suddenly while physical hunger comes on gradually. Insatiable cravings often come with emotional hunger. Those types of cravings will not come from true, physical hunger. Emotional hunger is never satisfied, but physical hunger can be satisfied.

Reminder: Techniques for Emotional Hunger

Whatever emotions you are experiencing, do not suppress them. Acknowledge these emotions. They are valid, but they do not need to rule over you.

Determine the type of emotion or feeling you are experiencing when you are tempted to eating only for emotional comfort. Perhaps the feeling is anger, sadness, disappointment, or jealousy. It can not be stressed enough that using a journal can help you navigate through your emotions. Once you are aware of the emotion and the cause for it, you can deal with it as needed. In the meantime, stay away from food until your emotions are under control.

If needed, talk to someone, or find an activity that relaxes you. Taking a walk helps with stress as well as squeezing a stress ball. Read, write, watch a movie, take a bath, play a game, or spend time with your family. Any activity is good as long as food is not involved.

What if you blow it?

Everyone makes mistakes. No human being on Earth is the perfect mindful eater. Part of mindfulness is learning the process. There is no judgment with mindful eating. Only altering or adjusting activities and actions as needed.

If you overeat, or if you slip up and eat when you are not hungry, simply try to find the behavior that caused you to do this. After that, wait until physical hunger before eating again. Most of all, be patient with yourself as well as the process.

Reminder: Eat at Set Times and Places

Once you establish a routine while eating, your body will follow. If your body is accustomed to eating at certain times a day, you will become hungry at those times. Remember this if you have an event planned. You can skip a meal, or eat a considerably less amount throughout the day of your event, then, you will be hungry and ready to eat when the time comes.

Always sit when eating. Unless there is some type of unforeseen circumstance, there is no good reason to be standing while eating. Remember, the more relaxed you are, the better you will enjoy your eating experience and avoid overeating.

Take the Process One Meal at a Time

Rome was not built in a day. Most of the time, it is impossible for people to decide on a given day that they will eat mindfully then accomplish the process perfectly that day. Give yourself time. Begin eating mindfully one meal at a time. Perhaps, to begin with, you will want to practice mindful eating for one meal a day until you feel more comfortable moving the process to your other meals during the day.

Bad habits did not develop in one day. With that in mind, it will take time for good habits to develop. When you begin changing the way you have been thinking about food, not to mention a mind pattern that has gone on for years, it will not change in a short period of time A mindful eater is persistent and does not give up.

Have More Than a Few Minutes to Eat

If you find that you are rushed to get to work on some mornings, and you are getting hungry but you have no time to eat, it might be a good idea to wait until you have time to enjoy your meal. Rushing the eating process has been one of the sources of eating issues. Developing the habit of giving yourself time to eat is a good one. If needed, take a few bites of toast or crackers to avoid becoming sick.

Use Utensils

Mindful eaters make a habit of using utensils even with foods that can be eaten using your hands. Utensils take a few extra minutes to use, but using them keeps you from rushing. Remember to put your fork or spoon down between bites. Cut your food into bite-size pieces to avoid taking large bites.

Food Choices

Although we have established that it is acceptable to have treats, choosing foods that will keep you full for a long period of time is essential. Protein is very sustaining. Carbohydrates give you energy. Healthy fats are good for cholesterol levels and heart disease. Dairy Products are a great source of calcium which is good for your bones.

While it is not necessary to count out your servings per day from these food groups, it is advisable to eat a variety of food with your meals. Do not stay in one food group. Variety is good for your body and pleasing to the taste buds.

Counting calories, fat grams, and carbs are not necessary with mindful eating. These dieting practices only frustrate you. They do very little to encourage mindfulness. A mindful eater observes her eating habits. She will adjust her food choices as she discovers the types of foods that help her body.

Give up Multitasking

Multitasking while eating will never be a good idea for the mindful eater. It is simply a distraction that will keep you from truly tasting and enjoying your food. Mindfulness brings awareness. We forget to taste and chew our food.

The problem with multitasking is not only that it causes you to miss tasting your food, but it also causes some other tasks to be half-done. Sometimes, we need to slow down our pace in life which will, in turn, help slow down our eating.

When you realize that you are trying to eat and do other tasks, simply stop and re-focus. If you are texting and eating, put your phone away. If you are watching television, turn it off. If you have books or papers with you while you are eating, put them away and focus on eating.

Reminder: Consider the Source

Considering the sources of your food brings gratefulness for your food which usually will cause you to enjoy it more. The sources of food range from those who grew and tended the crops, processed the food, to those who prepare our food. When you consider the source, you will begin to connect to your family which is always needful. Culture awareness is another way to consider the food source if you are eating foreign cuisine.

As a result of considering the source, you will become more grateful which will, in turn, create an appreciation of your meal. Usually, you will take more time with your eating which aids the mindful eating process. Having connections with your family and sharing meals with others will enhance mindful eating as well.

Reminder: Emotions Are Deceitful

Although you should never suppress your emotions, they can not be relied upon for an accurate guide when it comes to eating. Emotional highs and lows can lead you to binge eating, or overeating in general. Mindful eating will help you to distinguish emotional hunger from physical hunger.

It is essential that you find some way to deal with certain emotions. In the meantime, you can still practice mindful eating so that your emotions do not dictate your eating habits. Be sure you are finding productive ways to occupy your mind in between meals.

Know Your Emotional Triggers

If boredom sends you to the refrigerator, remember to have activities to keep your mind off food. For some, people eat when they are angry. Others eat when they are depressed. Eating out of elation is common. For me, all emotions brought the desire to eat so I had to find other ways to celebrate. Knowing your emotional triggers and planning ahead will prevent bouts of emotional eating.

Watch Your Thoughts

Always pay attention to your thoughts. Are they productive or destructive? Thinking negatively about yourself or the mindful eating process will accomplish nothing. Keep reminding yourself that you can eat mindfully. Keep negativity out of your thoughts, and do not listen to it from others.

While eating, keep your focus on what you are eating. If your thoughts drift, re-focus. When you are not eating, do not focus on food. There are other activities on which you can keep your focus. Where you place your focus is important. Thoughts easily become actions if not guarded.

Guarding your thoughts certainly is not easy. The process of mindful eating does require some work. Passivity is not your friend. Stay aware! Despite the great deal of effort required, the end is worth the means.

Reminder: Maintain Mindfulness

You might have progressed a long way in the mindful eating process, but you will have to maintain what you have achieved. The maintenance is not difficult if you stay with it; however, if you let down your guard, it could take a great deal of work to regain the ground again. Thinking productively on a regular basis will make it easier to notice when a thought is not in line with your pattern of thinking.

You Can Eat Without Guilt

You were meant for guilt-free eating. Enjoy your food! Eating was a process that was meant to bring you joy. There are a variety of reasons why people might feel guilt when they eat, but mindfulness will help you press past guilt and move on to the enjoyment of eating.

Approach Comfort Food with Caution

If you are truly hungry and are confident you can refrain from overindulging on a comfort food, you are free to eat it. Approach the food with caution since it has caused you problems in the past. You should not be eating comfort foods at every meal.

Resolve

Once you have become accustomed to mindful eating, each day must bring new resolve. Remaining in mindful eating will not happen by accident. You will have to purpose in your mind on a daily basis to not stray from mindful eating. Make determination an order of every day.

Most likely, time will have to be spent on a daily basis preparing your mind for mealtimes. You must never give up keeping your thoughts focused where they should be both during and in between meals. Thoughts become actions if they are not guarded. You will always have to be quick to put certain thoughts out of your mind and replace them with the better way of thinking.

Parties, Restaurants, and Other Social Functions

Many people will do well when they are practicing mindful eating at home. A major challenge is to learn to eat mindfully when eating out at restaurants, parties, and other social functions. The following are some tips for dining out:

- Arrive at the restaurant or function hungry but not ravenous.
- Have in mind what you are going to order or what you might select to eat at a party.
- Balance your meal. Choose a different variety of foods in small portions and on a small plate.
- Ask for a go-box ahead of time. Put at least half of your entree in the box.

• Share a meal with someone else. Restaurants serve large portions so there will be plenty for you both.

• Focus on eating when dining out just as you would at home. Do not allow yourself to become distracted.

• Stay hydrated. Sip between bites before, during, and after a meal.

In order to be hungry for these events, you might have to eat very little in the meals preceding your event. You could either skip a meal or, you could eat enough beforehand to take the edge off your hunger. With these steps, feelings of physical hunger will return quickly.

Now It Is Up to You

Now that this book is soon coming to a close, the decision is yours. You can choose to make a life-long practice of eating mindfully, or you stay where you have been. There is nothing that has been laid out in this book that is impossible for you to do if you are mindful. The goal is not beyond your grasp.

Keep *The Mindful Eating Bible: The Secret Mind Hack For Ending Binge Eating And Emotional Eating, Rediscovering A Healthy Relationship With Food, And Ending Your Life-long Battle With Weight Loss* as a guide in which to refer as time goes by. Rereading certain portions will bring reminders to you that will encourage you if you are feeling that you lack motivation. Keep a journal to write down anything that you need to process, or, anything that you feel keeps you going.

Starting an accountability group with people you know not only will help you, but it will also encourage others to make the same great decision as you. Accountability will keep you on track, and it is a great way to socialize with others and make new friends. Having someone to take the journey with you is meaningful.

Ditch Dieting

It is not recommended that you mix mindful eating with dieting. Confusion would be the order of the day. Do not waste your time or energy counting calories and fat grams as well as weighing and measuring your portions. Trust your body to give you the signals you need to judge hunger and fullness. As long as you are eating a variety of foods, you should be getting the nutrition that you need.

Treats

A food that you consider to be a treat should remain a treat as much as possible. If you have it every day, it is no longer a treat. Remember to eat a variety of foods with nutritional value that you truly enjoy.

Exercise

Mindful eating should be combined with regular exercise and drinking water. Your body will let you know when you need hydration. While it is fine to drink other beverages, drinking water is one of the best choices you can make. Exercise does not have to be strenuous. Walking is a great exercise and a good stress reliever; however, if you enjoy other types of exercise, by all means, get moving.

Additional Motivation

Never tell yourself that you can not eat mindfully. Keep your attitude positive. There will be days when you struggle, but struggling is where you learn and grow both as an individual and as a mindful eater. The mistakes that you make and from which you learn are tools that you can use to help guide you in making other decisions.

Encourage yourself and others. Be the shining light in your accountability group. If you encourage others, you will find that you will remain encouraged as well. By choosing to be part of an accountability group, you will have the opportunity to help others with the experience you have gained.

Now, make your choice, and resolve to eat mindfully for the rest of your life. When you fall, get back up, dust yourself off, and keep going. Once you begin to see the benefits of your choice, you will be glad you kept your resolve.

If you enjoyed and found this book valuable, please leave a short review on Amazon!

Final Words

Now that you have completed *The Mindful Eating Bible: The Secret Mind Hack For Ending Binge Eating And Emotional Eating, Rediscovering A Healthy Relationship With Food, And Ending Your Life-long Battle With Weight Loss*, please make others aware of its availability. So many people seem unable to maintain weight loss, or, they just are not able to lose weight at all. Food has a magnetic pull to which they seem drawn. Many want to be free from this pull. They just have no idea where to start. This book could help them as it has helped you.

Make mindful eating a part of your everyday. This eating plan can be successful for you even during holidays, birthdays, and other special occasions. The process of mindful eating, once complete, not only changes eating habits but people's lives. When people lose weight and become healthier, their lives change. They are able to do what they could not do before. Energy levels increase which enhances moods.

Mindfulness can overflow from your eating habits into other areas of your life as well. You can work mindfully, engage in relationships mindfully, and so much more! The journey of mindfulness can give you a new life.

Putting this book into the hands of everyone who struggles with overeating is the goal. Written to motivate and encourage people to aspire to positive changes in their lives, *The Mindful Eating Bible* and its message must reach the masses. Please help others find this guide to a healthy eating lifestyle.

Lifestyle changes come neither quickly nor easily. The fact that you took the time to go through the reading of this work indicates that you are ready for change. You are serious about making mindful eating a great part of your life. You are to be commended.

I appreciate you as the reader giving value to the contents of this book. Without you, works like this one could not be circulated. Thank you for taking the time to read.